*Rose & Roger*

*Jesus is Lord!*

## What People Are Saying about *The Hidden Kingdom...*

————◆◆◆————

Dr. Dale Fife has done it again! With his gift for narrative and the transparency of one whose passion is the pursuit of God's presence, he ushers the reader first into "An Audience with the King" and then "Into the Kingdom." The Scripture says, *"He who has ears, let him hear...."* To the reader, I declare, "He who reads, let him read...." The experience will change your life as you find yourself journeying from *The Secret Place* to *The Hidden Kingdom*.

—*Tommy Tenney*
Author, *The God Chasers*
President & CEO, GodChasers.network

What Dr. Fife offers us in *The Hidden Kingdom* is not a how-to book, but rather a "you-can-too" book. His unique ability and sensitivity to see things in the "hidden" world of the "upside-down" kingdom will bring fresh vision to your personal journey with the Lord.

—*Bishop Joseph L. Garlington, Sr., Ph.D.*
Senior Pastor, Covenant Church of Pittsburgh
Presiding Bishop, Reconciliation! Ministries International

This book is essential for those who want to get closer to the King and His kingdom. Discover the dimensions, the foundations, and the secrets of the invisible kingdom, and experience the joy of living there. Dale Fife does a great job of portraying the eternal kingdom in metaphoric parable.

—*LaMar Boschman*
Author, Musician, Worship Leader, Recording Artist
The Worship Institute

*Blessings*
*Dr. Dale C. Fife*

Much of today's church hides in isolation behind walls of separation from the world. How refreshing to receive vital, needed revelation that the church is to be the manifestation of the kingdom of God wherever we go. A friend of many years, Dr. Fife is especially gifted to "see" in the spirit realm. I know he is a man who walks in intimacy with the Lord. He's a modern mystic, whose accurate revelations uniquely align with the scriptural account of the Gospel of the kingdom.

This book will help liberate Christians who experience the irrelevance of isolation and launch them into the excitement of daily living here on earth as citizens in the kingdom of God, with the ultimate hope of life in the kingdom yet to come. It is timely revelation. I highly recommend that you read it, digest it, let it change your life.

—*Jim Erb*
Pastor, Pleasant Valley Church, Niles, Ohio
Overseer, Antioch International Ministries

Since the disciples asked Jesus two thousand years ago, Christians have sought answers about the kingdom of God. In the tradition of the church mystics of days past, Dr. Fife takes the reader on an adventure into a place removed from what we call time. There one will find a familiar reminiscence from journeys we too have taken. Familiar Scriptures come alive with color and dimension on each page, stirring up fresh longings to experience the Lord in His kingdom.

—*Ron A. MacDonald*
Academic Dean, All Africa Bible College
Durban, South Africa

"Once upon a time" are words that every child learns to hang on to with bated breath as their imaginations are prepared to take them on an adventure. Adults have those words deeply embedded in their consciousness, and every time they hear them, they reclaim the lost resources of their childhood and become young again, sitting on the edge of adventure.

Jesus, the Master Storyteller, impacted the hearts and minds of His listeners with what I like to call "parabolic speech." It is story, it is metaphor, and it puts you right into the event so that you can experience the experience of the experience for yourself.

Dale Fife is both a dear friend and a great man of God. He also happens to be a masterful storyteller as well as a powerful practitioner of spiritual truth and the demonstration of God's power. For Dale, intimacy with God is what it's all about. He stands today as one of God's vessels to bring about a restoration of kingdom truth and power by the subtle graces of symbol, image, metaphor, and even "once upon a time" kind of power.

The book you now hold in your hand is an adventure of a lifetime. Join this master storyteller as he takes you on a journey, a journey so seamless you won't know where the earthly story ends and heavenly reality begins. That is the way God has always wanted it to be.

Your life will be transformed simply by the experience of reading *The Hidden Kingdom*. What you do with what you experience will determine the level of transformation in those whom you touch because of it.

—*Mark J. Chironna, Ph.D.*
Author, Musician, Host on TBN-TV
Overseer, The Master's Touch International Church
Orlando, Florida

Forget your cliché-ridden definitions of the kingdom of God as the Holy Spirit breathes new life into that which has become worn or mundane. Experience a pendulum of emotions as you take this incredible journey into *The Hidden Kingdom*. Allow its truths to penetrate deep into your soul. You'll not only continue the walk that began in the well of His presence, but by the end of this book, you will also have learned how to walk with the Lord in *The Hidden Kingdom*.

—*Gary and Lynn Brooks*
In His Image Ministries
Candler, NC

After reading Dr. Fife's first book, *The Secret Place*, I looked forward with keen anticipation to his next one. From the first page on, I was captivated with *The Hidden Kingdom*. It brought me into an exciting awareness of the beauty, the greatness, and the wonder of our God. It made me want to spend more time in His presence. I was especially grateful for the frequent references to Scripture, which authenticate Dale's precious experiences with the Lord Jesus. *The Hidden Kingdom* is powerful and exciting reading. It made me say, "More, Lord, more!"

—*Rev. Karl E. Unger*
Pastor Emeritus, Judson Baptist Church
Burton, Michigan

Dale Fife's courageous words from his personal journal are a witness of how intimacy with Jesus can transform a life. This story had to be told to encourage others to walk as Enoch walked and to trust in their own visions. The lessons learned from *The Hidden Kingdom* will be a teaching tool for years to come. While reading this book, the scenes came alive to me, and I felt as though I were present in the story. This book will take the reader on a stimulating journey that leads to the discovery of God's love in a new and profound way.

—*Rev. Barbara Lachance*
Pastor, Teacher, International Speaker
Founder and President, Connecticut House of Prayer, Inc.

In a day of quick-fix, self-help, ten-easy-steps-for-every-thing mentality, Dr Fife has discovered a totally different approach to the Christian quest. His new book, *The Hidden Kingdom,* will awaken the longing cries of your heart for fellowship with the living God and will allow you to see that many of the answers you are seeking are found in Him. *The Hidden Kingdom* will reveal that the most significant thing you could do for yourself, your family, and your calling is to fellowship with God. Page by page as you read this book, you will encounter the Lord and become alive with a fresh love for Him. Whether you are a new believer in Christ or an established leader in His church, this book will unlock a hunger for God that will rearrange your entire world.

—*Vincent B. Manzo*
Senior Pastor, City of Hope International Church
Kearny, New Jersey

Imagine a church where every believer walks in the reality of God's kingdom, infused and transformed by the resurrection power of God. It is coming! Dale Fife's new book, *The Hidden Kingdom,* gives us a glimpse into this incredible future. He has powerfully and purposefully painted an inspired portrait of God's kingdom. This is raw revelation from the brush of intimacy.

Like Ezra in the days of Nehemiah, I believe that Dale is a modern-day scribe. He truly has applied *"the pen of a ready writer"* (Psalm 45:1) to the scroll for the purpose of equipping the saints. In *The Hidden Kingdom,* suddenly things come together in a seamless expression of God's government and purpose.

As you journey into the heart of God, you will find your own heart strangely warmed by God's anointing. Read and be changed!

—*Briskilla Zananiri*
Abana Ministries
Charlotte, NC

THE
# HIDDEN
# KINGDOM

JOURNEY INTO THE HEART OF GOD

# DR. DALE A. FIFE

W

WHITAKER
HOUSE

## THE HIDDEN KINGDOM: Journey into the Heart of God

For speaking engagements, you may contact the author at:
Dr. Dale A. Fife
The Potter's House
326 Brickyard Road
Farmington, CT 06032
e-mail: MnTopMin@aol.com

ISBN: 0-88368-947-2
Printed in the United States of America
© 2003 by Dr. Dale Arthur Fife

Whitaker House
30 Hunt Valley Circle
New Kensington, PA 15068
Website: www.whitakerhouse.com

Library of Congress Cataloging-in-Publication Data (pending)

1 2 3 4 5 6 7 8 9 10 11 12 13 14 / 12 11 10 09 08 07 06 05 04 03

# Acknowledgments

It would be presumptuous, even foolish, to write about journeying into God's eternal dimension and ignore the incredible riches of the authentic Christian mystics. They have tapped into the inexhaustible source of God's presence and unselfishly poured their experience into the empty cup of a thirsty church.

We Christians have often been guilty of disowning our spiritual ancestors and squandering our spiritual heritage for a fleeting bowl of emotional porridge.[1] This regrettable choice becomes obvious when we scan the shelves of the average bookstore. Much that is in print caters to the appetite of the masses for spiritual pabulum or seeks to appease the intellect. Most of the substantive writing regarding intimacy with God is limited to a few meager selections or consigned to the Catholic sections, who have encouraged and nurtured the intuitive nature of the Christian life within their protective womb.

I want to thank Bob Whitaker Sr., Bob Whitaker Jr., and all the staff at Whitaker House for helping to remedy this unacceptable situation. Your passion for spiritual substance is the beat of my own heart.

Once in a while a publishing house, like the one I am blessed to work with, will reprint something from the vaults of the past. These authors give us more than descriptions of the spiritual life; they are guides, spiritual directors who show us the way into His presence. Their writings have become the "classics" we look to for guidance on our own spiritual journeys. I will not attempt to list all these wonderful resources in case I overlook some, but if you search diligently, you will discover these hidden treasures for yourself. [2]

To these authors, both ancient and contemporary, I owe an enormous debt of gratitude. I remove my cap and salute these brave souls who went beyond the boundaries of the popular and accepted. It is their influence that fires and animates the body of Christ. Like them, we are called to abandon ourselves to the Lord.

However, in case you might get the wrong impression, let me hasten to thank the theologians who labored with keen intellect and dogmatic relentlessness to catalog and communicate the truth of the Scriptures and shape them into a system of doctrine and belief. Frank X. Tuoti eloquently summed up the need for balance in these words:

> All genuine Christian mysticism must be grounded in sound theology lest it run the real risk of being a self-styled kind of counterfeit mysticism. Conversely, there can be no true theology without the experiential ingredient of mysticism. [3]

To those teachers who helped me discover the truth regarding the kingdom—E. Stanley Jones, John Sanford, Ern Baxter, George Eldon Ladd, Gerhardus Vos, Richard Akeroyd, and Bob Mumford, to name a few—thank you for your deliberate, faithful scholarship.

To the school of the prophets, whose company I am most comfortable in, thank you for your sacrificial obedience. These men and women dare to declare and record what they have seen through the eyes of the Spirit. Tommy Tenney, Rick Joyner, Bishop Bill Hammond, Peter Wagner,

Cindy Jacobs, Sharon Stone, Gary Brooks, Mark Chironna, Morton Kelsey, James Erb, Mark Virkler, Francis Frangipane, Jim Goll, and Ken Gire are a few of the spiritual heroes in my personal hall of fame.

The church often portrays its faith through the creative arts. Painting, in particular, is one of the most powerful avenues of expression. Indeed, a picture is worth a thousand words. Amanda Adendorff, a South African born Messianic Jew, is a talented and spiritually perceptive painter to whom I am deeply grateful. Thanks, Mandy, for your remarkable ability to capture the prophetic vision of *The Hidden Kingdom* on canvas.[4]

Last but not least, to my covenant friend, Bishop Joseph Garlington: You refuse to be satisfied with the status quo. You are a man who will not accept anything less than a full manifestation of God's kingdom, where race and gender do not divide and God is no respecter of persons. Your passion has ignited my own heart. You are the one who took my hand as a fledgling pilgrim and led me up the mountain of spiritual experience to a higher plane than I thought capable of reaching. Your encouragement to keep climbing when I wanted to stop has enabled me to see from a vista that is astounding. We are brothers in the Spirit, embracing *The Hidden Kingdom* of our Lord. Thank you, Joseph.

This book is affectionately dedicated
to our two sons,
**Scott and Brian,**
who were taught at an early age
to seek first the kingdom of God
and His righteousness.

# Contents

# Foreword

## by Bishop Joseph Garlington

I was riding behind the "copilot" of a Jamaican bus driver who was seeking to steer our bus through a very narrow place, when it seemed as though the mirror on our side of the bus was going to have a collision with a post that was less than a hair's breadth away. I was both startled and amused by the sudden shout of warning that filled the bus with his rich West Indian accent: "Small up yourself, Mon. Small up yourself!"

I have since heard that admonition on several occasions when seeking to understand some obscure statement in the Scriptures or when I've been feeling just a little bit more pompous in certain arenas than the Holy Spirit could accept. I believe it is the "hidden secret" to *The Hidden Kingdom.* Furthermore, I'm even more convinced as I read the incredible insights Dr. Fife shares with us in this book, as well as in *The Secret Place,* that he has succeeded in "smalling up" himself. Let me tell you why.

When Dale Fife's first book, *The Secret Place,* touched the Christian community, there was an immediate and electric response from believers who had personally experienced similar adventures in prayer—but they had been reluctant to share them. *The Secret Place* did two things: it validated the genuine moments many believers (particularly intercessors) had in their prayer times, and it emboldened others (not necessarily intercessors) to pursue a deeper relationship with the Father, Son, and Holy Spirit through extended seasons of fellowship.

Years ago, Dale and I delighted in a word game that we often played while driving around the city of Pittsburgh or other places as we traveled together. We would both look at the name on a street sign and then challenge the other to say the name backwards. Needless to say, the outcomes would often be hilarious and, once in a while, amazing. Yet, more often than not, Dale would be able to see the reverse order before any of the rest of us. I share this because that unique ability of his in the natural world seems to parallel his ability and sensitivity to see things in the "hidden" world, which is sometimes called the "upside-down" kingdom.

Today, Christianity seems to have a growing antagonism about anything that tends toward mystical overtones, and yet those of us who accept the reality of these experiences and are comfortable with them contend that the unseen world is more real, more vast, and far more substantive than the world of our day-to-day experience. Pierre Teilhard de Chardin summed it up very nicely for us when he said, "We are not human beings having a temporary spiritual experience; we are spiritual beings having a temporary human experience."

I am absolutely convinced that the "hidden" key to understanding the "hidden things" is becoming childlike. In fact, Jesus Himself revealed that truth to His disciples when they overheard Him giving thanks to His Father for what He realized the Father has entrusted to the Lord's disciples:

> *At that very time He rejoiced greatly in the Holy Spirit, and said, "I praise You, O Father, Lord of heaven and*

*earth, that You have hidden these things from the wise and intelligent and have revealed them to infants. Yes, Father, for this way was well-pleasing in Your sight."*
(Luke 10:21)

Quantum physicists of today accept without argument the existence of phenomena that are both small and infinite; they submit themselves to the phenomena, and it seems as though they ask the phenomena, "What are you?" However, on the larger plane of the kingdom of God—a profoundly spiritual dimension—the theologians of today want the hidden phenomena of God's kingdom not only to submit to them, but also to let them dictate what it can or cannot be. The modern-day church is actually living an "experience-poor" life, which has produced an anemic spirituality. The vigorous and dynamic spiritual experience that is so very prominent in the third-world revivals is noticeably absent in the Western world.

We must summarily reject the growing and insipid form of Christianity that denies the present reality of miracles, visions, and dreams simply because "they are not for today." This is often the argument cited by those who have either never experienced significant moments in God that touched the numinous or were warned against having them by others. A godly businessman once told Dr. Howard Ervin, "A man with an experience is not at the mercy of a man with an argument."

> "A man with an experience is not at the mercy of a man with an argument."

Dr. Fife is a man with an experience. He is also a man of the Word, with a strong background and training in formal study. He is no stranger to controversy, because his love of God and his hunger for more of Him has driven him to his knees for answers on more than one occasion. This childlike posture has qualified him to be a recipient of *"things...revealed...to infants."*

Tommy Tenney once shared with me that a mentor told him, "The secret place is a secret every time!" What I now share with you as the open secret of Dale's inner journeys in both *The Secret Place* and *The Hidden Kingdom* is that a long time ago he learned the secret revealed in the admonition of that Jamaican copilot: "Small up yourself, Mon. Small up yourself!"

What Dr. Fife offers us in *The Hidden Kingdom* is not a how-to book, but rather a "you-can-too" book. Don't approach this book as a critical scholar but as a seeking learner. Ask the Holy Spirit to teach you the principles He wants you to learn from Dale's journey. Then put what is uniquely special and edifying into practice in your own personal walk with Him.

—*Bishop Joseph L. Garlington, Sr., Ph.D.*
Senior Pastor, Covenant Church of Pittsburgh
Presiding Bishop, Reconciliation! Ministries International

# Introduction

The world you are about to enter is filled with dreams and visions. It is a place where symbolism transcends logic and image conveys truth in such clarity that it captivates our souls and penetrates our spirits. This mysterious milieu is a realm of sign and shadow that draws us into the presence of the Almighty, where things must be seen with spiritual eyes and can be perceived only by a believing heart.

Chances are, if you truly are a spiritual pilgrim in search of the living God, you have crossed the border into this realm already. Like most people, you stumble through its regions groping for some tangible, down-to-earth walking stick to stabilize your journey. Your

> Here is a place where symbolism transcends logic and image conveys truth with such clarity that it penetrates our spirits.

guidebook is the Bible, but you soon discover that it is replete with types and symbols, visions and dreams.[1] These road signs in God's kingdom are often mysterious and shadowy, not a true likeness of the object they represent in all respects. If they were, they would no longer be types or symbols, but the object itself. (See Hebrews 8:4–5; 10:1.)

The Bible speaks in images, parables, and stories, but our tendency is to look for the true-or-false sections that cater to our technical mind-set. We savor the self-help and how-to chapters as we try to find "the" formula: three easy, universal steps to overcome life's struggles. [2]

Alas, perceiving the spiritual dimension cannot occur on a purely rational level since spiritual reality itself is not limited to the logical realm. It requires images, not just concepts. It is through internalizing the meaning of symbols rather than through logical reasoning that change takes place within us. Granted, God does not intend for us to discard our intellect, but it is only one way of comprehending reality. Images, on the other hand, provide a language of the soul, a dialect of the imagination, which arouses our sensitivity to the spiritual world. [3]

> Images provide a language of the soul, a dialect of the imagination, which arouses our sensitivity to the spiritual world.

We make and use images far more than we realize. They form and guide us. We interpret our worldview with metaphors, similes, and analogies. Flags, corporate logos, symbols-only highway signs, colors, and objects take on meaning and nuances that transcend the literal.

Even our words are mere symbols, which represent an inner world of thought and perception. They are charged with connotation that far exceeds the *Oxford English Dictionary* definition. Meaning is cultural, and sometimes so personal, that a single word can trigger an explosion of emotion or thought that goes far beyond the intended meaning. No wonder communication is so often difficult.

Because the human spirit belongs to the unseen realm, we are forced to explore its mysteries by the dim light of symbols and images. We must cease from being theologians, intellectual surgeons dissecting God and the soul, and enter into the realm of imagination. It is here in this misty world of shadows that the poet, artist, musician, and dreamer see with clarity. We must trust their vision and follow their lead. [4]

The church is like an audience gathered in a theater. We eagerly anticipate the beginning of the movie, but suddenly we realize that the film is three-dimensional. At first we strain to bring the image displayed on the screen into focus, but to no avail. Many give up in frustration and leave the building to pursue more easily discerned messages. Those of us who refuse to walk out soon realize that we need special glasses. Suddenly, as the picture becomes clear, the theater comes alive with the shouts and movements of the audience. Viewers literally reach into the air to try to touch the intangible images leaping off the screen or duck down to avoid them. "Did you see that?" we ask each other in wonder and delight. Those who still can't see think we're crazy.

It takes vision to perceive spiritual reality. Vision is much more than an unseen force that motivates us to achieve or the ability to see into the future. Vision is the "God-view" made known to the mortal mind. It is the ability to see as God sees.

> Vision is the "God-view" made known to the mortal mind.

Vision gives us the ability to discern the eternal implications in the present situation, to interpret the events or circumstances of life within the framework of God's purpose. It is the eyeglass through which the patriarchs, prophets, and seers peered. It is what inflamed the hearts of Jesus' disciples and ignited the early church. It is the privilege of every born-again, Spirit-filled believer.

It was Solomon, the wisest man who ever lived, who said, *"Where there is no vision, the people are unrestrained"* (Proverbs 29:18). The word *vision* in this context can be understood to mean "prophetic revelation." Vision, then, is an inspired look at reality, the supernatural ability to focus on a blurred world and see it through the eyes of God.

Yet, far more important than our ability to make sense of this material world is our desperate need to see the invisible world that exists inside of us within the human spirit. Many pass through life ignoring its existence. It is an inner world of silence and solitude, yet it screams for attention, yearning to be explored. It is the emptiness within us, waiting to be filled with His presence.

Here in this non-space is where the kingdom of God is discovered and realized. Yet, only a few ever find their way into it, most having disregarded the invitation extended to them. (See Matthew 7:13–14; 22:1–14.) Those who brave this spiritual dimension soon come to understand the realm of the inner world and learn to speak in its language. [5]

> The insights we garner through the language of prophetic revelation become compass points that lead us to Him!

A wonderfully creative diversity exists in the language of the heart. It should not surprise us that vision and dreams characterize this variety. God's gift of imagination is the marvelous ability to envision what is not seen with the natural eye. The Holy Spirit is brilliant in His ability to communicate through the anointed imagination. He uses many avenues to express the same spiritual truth. You may experience God's presence and receive revelation in an entirely different way than someone else does. God may use totally different words, images, and symbols to communicate His heart to you.

Our goal is not to sort through the language of symbols and images in order to establish their authenticity or credibility like spiritual cartographers making a celestial map. Rather, the purpose in the Father's heart is for us to understand the principles and spiritual truths conveyed by the variety of inspired pictures that the Holy Spirit chooses to communicate with. The insights that we garner through the language of prophetic revelation become compass points that lead us to Him!

This book is the account of one man's subjective journey into God's kingdom. It is the result of my passionate pursuit of His presence. I gladly acknowledge my weaknesses. I claim no special inspiration. I am not saying, "This is the way it is!" Rather, I'm saying, "This is the way I saw it in the Spirit!" My sole desire is to be faithful to the Lord Jesus Christ and His Word. Without apology, I hold fast to the inerrancy and infallible inspiration of the Holy Scriptures. The Bible is the only absolute standard by which this, and all prophetic revelation, must be tested and judged.

I invite you now to come along with me on a spiritual journey into His kingdom, past the world of pews and stained glass windows, clear of the impediments of religious externals, into God's eternal dimension, where the language is symbolic and spiritual vision is paramount. Our journey begins in the well of His presence, in *The Secret Place.* [6]

Truly, truly I say to you,
unless one is born again,
he cannot *see* the kingdom of God.

...

Unless one is born of water
and the Spirit, he cannot *enter*
the kingdom of God.

—*Jesus*

# Part One:

# An Audience
# with the King

chapter one

# This Is the Air I Breathe

---◆◆◆◆◆---

Anticipation filled our days with excitement; our son and his wife were expecting their third child. The birth of a grandchild is normally a joyous occasion, but this birth was truly a miracle. Out of the wrenching pain of a marriage almost shipwrecked on the jagged rocks of life's disappointments and heartache came the quiet whisper of the promise of new life.

## The Prodigal

For seven long years, our son Brian abandoned the Lord's call on his life. Like the New Testament Prodigal, he squandered his spiritual inheritance and destiny. The church disappointed him. Christian leaders and ministries failed him, their hypocritical lives portraying righteousness, while all along they lived a hidden life of sin and self-serving deception. When finally their duplicity was exposed, Brian was left to pick up the pieces. What had begun in the heart of this young man as hopeful, heartfelt zeal to serve God had culminated in his disillusionment. The gut-wrenching pain that gripped our son's life was so deep that he was sick in his soul.

He sought to drown his heartache in the pursuit of worldly pleasures and alcohol. Discarding his role as a husband and father, he spent his hours in the bars or lost himself in the woods hunting and fishing with his friends. Night after night for weeks at a time, his wife sat alone at their home in Pennsylvania wondering where he was or if he would ever come home. Lorrie spent her days waiting and longing for the man she had married to find himself again.

The pain of Brian's absence was soon reflected in the lives of our grandchildren, Aaron and Brianne, as they watched their daddy drown himself in things that kept him from them. He became a shadow in the house. There was no affection or affirmation that a daughter longs for, no companionship that a son needs from his father. Even when Brian was home, his emotional pain made him unresponsive to their needs.

> We gathered friends and intercessors to stand with us to save our son and his family.

Eunice and I watched in horror as our son slowly and steadily moved deeper and deeper into a sea of depression. Although we lived in Connecticut and couldn't often see Brian, we stormed heaven with our prayers. We gathered friends and intercessors to stand with us to save our son and his family. We cried out to God in desperation as only mothers and fathers can do when they see their children suffering and in pain.

One black night in November, the shroud of darkness engulfed Brian and finally brought him to the brink of total despair. The red pickup truck sped down the darkened country road. To the left, a single farmhouse window cast a muted light on the dampened roadway. A horrible screeching of tires suddenly shattered the quiet serenity of the countryside. An explosion of twisting metal and tearing steel lit up the night sky and thundered through the fog-covered fields as the speeding truck careened off the road and slammed into a utility pole. The driver was killed instantly. He was Brian's best friend. When Brian arrived at the accident scene several hours later, all that was left were scraps of metal and a few of his friend's construction tools scattered across the darkened field.

For Brian, the following weeks were filled with emotional pain that ached beyond description. Life no longer seemed to be worth living. Even his marriage didn't seem to warrant the effort needed to maintain it anymore. It was over. Our hearts broke as he told us he was filing for divorce. When he moved out of the house, we watched helplessly as Lorrie and the children clung tenaciously to the slim hope that God would intervene.

## A Desperate Cry

Unknown to us, Brian was desperately crying out to God from the emotional jail that held him prisoner. His plea came from deep within his soul. In torment one night, he lay on his back in an open field in the Pennsylvania countryside that he loved. Hidden in the tall grass of the isolated field, he looked up into the heavens with tear-filled eyes. He didn't whisper; he shouted with all the force he could muster. It was the heart-cry of a man, angry

> There was no audible voice, no thunder in the heavens, but something moved in eternity.

and alone, longing for his Creator, a cry of lostness and desperation that demanded a response.

"God, if You're real," He shouted, each word rumbling up from the angry ache inside, "If You care about me, please say something, God! Speak to me. Somehow, let me know that You care. I can't bear this pain any longer!"

There was no audible voice, no thunder in the heavens, but something moved in eternity. Whenever God hears this kind of cry, He *always* answers. Something began to change. Unseen forces were put in motion that stirred the grace, mercy, and compassion in the heart of God. But the change was not immediately manifested.

Brian was living a few doors away from his family in the house of a dear pastor who graciously took him in. One afternoon, my wife and I watched from the upstairs window of this friend's home as little Brianne came running down the country road from her house up the street, disregarding her parents' constant warnings to stay off the busy roadway. She charged into the house without knocking, flung her coat on a nearby chair, and without a word, declaratively spread her schoolbooks on the kitchen table.

My wife watched with a grandmother's breaking heart. She understood perfectly. Brianne was acting out the pain she felt as a little girl whose father had left home. Her actions clearly stated, "Wherever my daddy is, that's where I want to be. I'll do whatever it takes."

> Only a will that is surrendered to God brings about the inner peace we are searching for.

At that very moment, Brian was on his way out the door to see the attorney regarding divorce papers. When he was confronted with his daughter's longing face, his eyes were suddenly opened. He drove away in his black pickup, but he never made it to the lawyer's office. On the way, the Lord spoke to Brian, and he stopped to call Lorrie from a pay phone. "God has shown me that what I am doing is so wrong," he explained. "I just can't go through with this. Can we talk?"

Brian had finally heard God's voice. It came in such an unexpected way, but it was loud and clear. There was no escaping God's call upon his life, despite the shortcomings of the church or the human frailty of its leaders. At last, the surrender of his will to God brought the inner peace that Brian was searching for. It wasn't so much life's circumstances or other people that figured in his destiny. It was the cry of his heart for intimacy with God, for a man-to-God relationship that satisfies the deepest longings of the human soul, which finally brought resolution.

Brian wasn't the least bit interested in church or in religion. He had tasted that, and he had no desire to go back to that emptiness. He wanted a no-nonsense, sold-out relationship with the Almighty. With unbridled zeal, he cast himself on God's mercy. It was settled once and for all: "Oh, God, I surrender my life to the pursuit of Your will."

## Amazing Grace

The transformation was truly amazing. Brian rediscovered his first love. Instead of spending time away from the family, now he was always at home. Even more amazing, he couldn't stop reading the Bible. Instead of watching television, he spent time reading Christian books aloud to his family. Every opportunity that we had to be together, Brian would sit and ask me questions about the Lord. We discussed the Scriptures as a father and son. It was such a joy to me. He was hungry for God, and his thirst for spiritual truth was insatiable.

## New Life

Then, one day, Brian and Lorrie gave us the news, "Mom and Dad, we're pregnant!"

The announcement came as a complete shock. A multitude of thoughts scrolled through my mind. *Another grandchild! I wonder if it's a boy or a girl? Lord, You're so awesome. We almost lost this marriage, and now You are blessing it with another child.*

I guess I felt a little like Zacharias the priest, the husband of Elizabeth and the father of John the Baptist. I was going about my daily duties, tending to the burning of incense in the temple, when suddenly, quite unexpectedly, God showed up with the news that a child would be born. Disbelief clouded my thinking. *Could it be true?* I wondered. *Has God really come to bless our family with new life and purpose after we barely survived what seemed like imminent destruction?* He was giving us another life to care for. *This is powerfully prophetic*, I realized. Like Zacharias, I was speechless.

The coming months were filled with excitement and joyous anticipation. All the preparations were made for the arrival of this precious gift from God. The very thought of his arrival reminded me of what I often tell other parents: "The birth of a child is God's way of saying that life is good."

## Something Is Wrong

During Lorrie's pregnancy, Eunice and I visited Brian and his family and had several days of wonderful fellowship with them. When we were preparing to leave, Brian had gone to work, and we were standing on the front porch with Lorrie and Brianne saying our final goodbyes before heading back to Connecticut. The November afternoon sun was still quite warm, and we were anticipating a pleasant drive home.

"Before you go, please pray for me," Lorrie asked with a troubled expression, patting her protruding belly affectionately. "I don't feel right. I keep thinking something is wrong."

Lorrie was still months away from her delivery date, and we prayed in faith for God's protection over her and the child in her womb, asking the Lord to bless her with health and peace. After a few words of reassurance, we got in the car, drove out of their driveway, and headed east toward home. It never occurred to us to turn our cell phone on.

Before we had reached the town limits, Lorrie was standing in a pool of liquid. Her water had broken, and the baby was in serious trouble. She realized that she must get to a doctor immediately.

Hustling Brianne into the car, she sped to her doctor's office. The physician quickly confirmed her fears. "You need to get to the hospital immediately," she said. "This is very serious!"

After all that she had been through—the anguish of seeing her husband struggle for survival, the agonizing days and nights of wondering whether they would make it through the storm, the hours of crying out to God in an all-out fight to save her marriage, the excruciating process of overcoming the heartbreaking feelings of rejection and the awful pain of inferiority and failure—now she had another crisis to face.

"How could this be happening, God?" she cried in dismay. "Just when everything finally seems to be going our way!" She couldn't hold back the tears any longer.

> "It's okay, Mommy. It's going to be okay."

Brianne reached out to touch her mother's arm. "It's okay, Mommy," she said. "It's going to be okay."

The hospital was only a few blocks away. She was whisked into an examination room. The prognosis was not good. Labor had begun; she was already having contractions. The medical team acted without hesitation. "We will have to transfer you to a women's hospital in Pittsburgh. We don't have the necessary equipment here to sustain a baby this premature with such undeveloped lungs."

Brian walked into the emergency room in his work clothes to hear the distressing news. "Go!" he said. "I'll take care of the children and meet you at the hospital in Pittsburgh."

The ambulance raced toward the city. Lorrie felt more alone and scared than she had ever felt before. The children were gone, Brian was gone, and now she was speeding toward the unknown future, trying to cling to those few, reassuring words of her nine-year-old daughter, "It's okay, Mommy. It's going to be okay."

The hospital room was filled with the whirring, buzzing, and clicking of medical equipment. The fetal monitors accurately recorded the slightest change in the baby's condition. Comforted somewhat by the availability of the latest technology, Lorrie was further encouraged by Brian's arrival, but the unborn baby was by no means out of danger. Eventually, the medical team assigned her to a room. It looked as if she wasn't going to deliver during the night.

With the dawning of a new day, there seemed to be evidence that birth was not far away. She was wheeled into the birthing room where she spent the entire day. It was all to no avail. The child refused to be born.

Back in her room, the physicians continued to monitor Lorrie. If she could hold off delivery for a week, the baby's lung development would be significantly greater. His chances of survival would be much better. However, the risk of infection if he stayed in the womb increased with every hour. He could die from contagion.

## Prayer and Faith

Brian and Lorrie clung tightly to God in faith for the next several days. They passed the hours together, reading the Bible out loud. During mealtimes Brian ate in the cafeteria and then went to pray in the hospital chapel. At the end of each day, after the hospital's main entrance was closed, he pushed Lorrie to the hospital foyer in a wheelchair. She sat playing the beautiful grand piano by the front door while they worshipped the Lord together. Their songs of intercession and tender praise filled the hospital corridors with God's presence. Despite the critical nature of their circumstances, each moment was a sweet time of intimacy with each other and with Jesus.

Miraculously, an entire week passed by without the baby being born. Lorrie was scheduled to deliver on Tuesday morning. The ultrasound was disconcerting, though. She had felt a lot of movement, and the photographs confirmed that the baby had turned breech. Now the risks were even higher because a C-section would have to be performed. But God's prayer warriors were on assignment. At the very moment Lorrie sat in the examining room, her pastor was praying upstairs in the hospital for God's healing and protection.

## It's in God's Hands

A heavyset, elderly black woman, wearing socks that had "I love Jesus" printed on them, broke the silence. From her own wheelchair next to Lorrie in the ultrasound waiting room, she said, "Hon-ee, if there's no choice for you to make, then it's in God's hands."

Lorrie realized that these words from a total stranger were a message from the Lord, and she immediately bowed her head. "All along the way, Lord, there have been small miracles. But now, Jesus, we need a big one."

"This is your daddy speaking. Turn around!"

Delivery was scheduled for the next morning. Throughout the night, the fire of prayer was kept burning brightly. At one point, Brian gently laid his hand on Lorrie's tummy and spoke to the child in the womb. "This is your daddy speaking. Turn around!" he commanded with fatherly authority.

35

The time had come. It was in God's hands. One more ultrasound was taken. The medical staff was astounded. The baby had turned during the night! The likelihood of this happening was nothing short of miraculous. The lack of fluid in the womb made movement extremely difficult. The amniotic sac was clinging to the baby like a wet T-shirt, making his turning inside of the womb almost impossible. Obviously, this child was an overcomer!

## Ear First

Asa Jeremiah was born at 7:00 A.M. He came out *ear first*. The birthing room was packed with medical personnel. Even the medical students and other staff members who had stayed after their shift change to witness the birth cheered when the little guy made his way into this world.

For a brief moment, Lorrie got to see the baby. He struggled very hard to breathe, his premature lungs straining to take in air. He cried as he exerted almost all his energy to gasp for the breath of life. "If we don't get help for him to breathe right now, he will wear out and die within hours," the doctor said. And with that, Asa was rushed away to intensive care.

## Supernatural Breath

Buttons, tubes, switches, and wires surrounded the tiny incubator in the neonatal intensive care room. A monitor carefully gauged the performance of little Asa's vital functions. He had weighed four pounds, five ounces at birth. His weight had now dropped to three pounds, thirteen ounces. Like an astronaut totally dependent upon his spaceship for life, tiny Asa existed within his own earthbound life support system, a newcomer to the hostile atmosphere of earth.

The ache in Lorrie's heart was excruciating. She wanted to hold her son, to draw him close to her breast and comfort him, to welcome him into this world with the loving embrace of a mother. But she was denied access.

She sat beside the incubator in her hospital gown, looking through the glass walls at little Asa. He was small enough to hold in one hand. Taking every medical precaution, she carefully opened the small door on the side of the incubator. She reached in to touch the velvety skin of her little son. Her finger stroked his tiny back; a single fingertip completely filled his miniature hand. The touch was intimate, mother to son.

Yet, something else was evident. Another invisible presence filled the room. She knew He was there. Lorrie spontaneously began to sing.

> This is the air I breathe,
> This is the air I breathe,
> Your holy presence,
> Living in me. [1]

The words drifted through the antiseptic air of the intensive care unit and made their way into the presence of God. The song was a prayer. It was all she had to offer. It was the cry of a mother's heart for her child, who was struggling for the very breath of life. It was a declaration of faith and also a surrender of little Asa's life to the God who had given it to him in the first place.

She continued,

> This is my daily Bread,
> This is my daily Bread.
> Your very Word,
> Spoken to me.

And then, with every fiber of her being, she sang unashamedly from the very deepest part of her soul.

37

And I,

I'm desperate for You.

I'm lost without You...

With each word, the realization of God's powerful mercy overwhelmed her like giant waves of glory.

"Oh, God, You gave me back my husband. You spared little Asa's life. You are the air I breathe," she whispered. "Your very presence lives in me. This is my prayer, Lord. Never take Your presence from us. All of our days we will sing Your praise. Let every breath that Asa takes be the breath of Your presence. Thank You for giving me back my family. Thank You for restoring my husband. Without You, Jesus, we cannot live."

## The Cry of Every Heart

The song hasn't ceased. The melody and the lyrics continue. These heartfelt words of utter dependence on God have become the constant cry of our family. It's my very own song! But it is far more than our special song. I believe that it is the heart-cry of every man and woman born into this world. Whether you realize it or not, it's your song, too.

Oh, God, we're desperate for You! We are lost without You! Your holy presence living in us is what life is about. Like Asa, we are born with gasping lungs, and without You, God, we cannot breathe. You are the oxygen of our lives. Your presence is the atmosphere of existence.

## We Hunger for the Secret Place

It is this passion and longing that drives us to the secret place where He dwells. This is the motive that compels us to pursue Him with absolute determination. He is the air we breathe. His holy presence is what the high priest sought in the Holy of Holies. Intimacy with Him is what the patriarchs and prophets hungered for. It is the essence and purpose of life. We are born to have intimacy with God. Our lives were designed for life in His kingdom.

We are all born "ear first." Our spirits are poised to listen for His voice from the moment we are conceived. He made us for Himself. God wants someone to talk with. That someone is each and every one of us!

The cry of Brian's heart was for intimacy with God. God answered that plea. The cry of Asa's lungs was, "Lord, You are the air I breathe." God also answered that cry, and Asa lived. Every life resonates with the same melody. The longing in our hearts remains steadfast. Our determination should be resolute: "We will seek You, Lord, and commune with You in the secret place."

## Growing in God

Asa is older now and quite healthy. He is an overcomer just like all of those who purpose to seek God's face. Place your ear close to His presence. He wants to speak to you. Prepare yourself for the journey ahead, the journey of a life that passionately pursues God's presence, purpose, and power. He wants you to be an overcomer, too. But first you must learn to listen.

chapter two

# Learning to Listen

————◆◆◆◆————

Heavy clouds blanketed the New England sky, totally
obscuring the sun from our valley. *This gloominess
certainly mirrors how I feel*, I thought, peering out
of the icy windshield at the wintry scene. The frigid late-
morning air created a trail of white puffs from the hot
engine exhaust behind me as I threaded my way through the
quiet residential streets toward the nearby church. During
the night, sand had been scattered over the roadway to
improve traction. The bitter cold made it sound as if spilled
graham cracker crumbs were crunching under my tires.

"I really don't want to do this today," I grumbled. I was
acting more out of a sense of duty than heartfelt intention.
The valley pastors were meeting, and I had procrastinated
leaving for the gathering as long as I could. I was uncom-
fortably late. Although my life has been wonderfully blessed
over the years as a result of meeting with my colleagues
in ministry, now I found myself struggling with a tangle
of emotions. A deeper issue, much more personal, ate away
inside of me. My spirit was troubled.

## A Gentle Rebuke

Intimacy with the Lord is the purpose and joy of my life, and the thought of the solitude of my warm cozy study lured me back home. I wanted to spend time alone with Jesus, walking with Him as Enoch walked with God. [1] *My time with You must be more important than this meeting,* I thought, the words pulling at my emotions.

Instantly, the Lord began to speak to me through a vision. The beautiful setting of the well of His presence flashed into my mind. I saw the low fieldstone wall that encircled the well's opening. Two wooden posts attached to the top of the wall extended upward to support a small, peaked roof. This roof provided shade and protection for the well. All around the well were brilliant rays of sunlight. Its water was cool and clear, again beckoning me to draw refreshing water out of its depths. [2]

> I wanted to spend time alone with Jesus, walking with Him as Enoch walked with God.

This is where I always go in the Spirit to meet with Him. But there was something notably different about the well this time, something that troubled me. A thick green patch of moss grew right next to the well in the very spot where I had stood for the past several months during the unfolding of the revelation that I record in my book *The Secret Place.*

The Holy Spirit rebuked me. My heart was pierced. I understood the message clearly; I was falling back into the same habit of neglect that had plagued me before. It had been only a few days since I had spent time in His presence, but already the life-giving freshness of intimacy with Him was beginning to fade. Despite my longing for communion with God and the sheer joy of walking with Him, I was neglecting the secret place again. I was allowing other things to take priority. This vision was a clear and alarming warning from God, a wake-up call for me to seek His face. *I must get back to the well of His presence,* I thought.

I quickly realized why I was torn between the desire to spend time alone with Him and the sense of duty I felt toward my fellow pastors. I wanted to turn the car around and head back home as quickly as possible, but something inside kept nudging me forward toward the meeting. Little did I realize that it was the Lord who had placed this gathering on my schedule. I was headed for a divine appointment.

"All right, Lord," I said, as I yielded to the inner voice of the Holy Spirit. "I repent of my negligence. I sense that You want me to go to this meeting, but I can't wait to get back to the secret place. As soon as I get home, I'll meet You at the well. I promise!"

## Should I Tell Them?

The medium-sized rectangular room was similar to those you find in churches everywhere, plain and wooden. Several folding tables were pushed together to form a larger surface. A large coffeemaker gurgled away on a cart next to one wall. Throwing my coat over a chair on the window side of the table, I filled a Styrofoam cup with steaming, black coffee. Its rich aroma helped to waken my senses as I took my seat.

"Well, Dale, what's going on with you?" The question caught me totally by surprise. I wasn't even sure who asked it. And then the room fell silent.

> "Lord, should I tell them about the secret place?"

It felt as if a bolt of lightning had hit me. I looked up from the table, my eyes slowly scanning the faces of my fellow pastors. "Lord," I whispered, "should I tell them about the secret place?" I struggled to control the tears that were forming in the corners of my eyes.

*"What's happening, Lord?"* I cried, and then the fountain of my soul was uncapped.

For the next fifteen minutes, the words poured out from the depths of my heart. "I've experienced the most incredibly sweet time of intimacy with the Lord. It's been going on now for months," I explained. "It all started with a simple prayer. One morning I said to the Lord, 'I want to be like Enoch, Jesus. I want to walk with You and be Your friend.' He answered that prayer. I'm sure He knows it's the cry of my heart.

"I find myself sitting in His presence for hours at a time. Sometimes the weight of His glory is so heavy that I have to bow my head. I can hardly see to write in my journal because of the tears that fill my eyes. The things that He is teaching me are overwhelming. I can't wait to spend time with Him every day."

## His Presence Enables Us

In that instant, Moses' life flashed before me. Surrounded by my fellow pastors, I suddenly realized what made Moses unique. God chose him to shepherd an entire nation. It was his encounter with the flaming bush that sent this broken shepherd from the shoeless holy ground of God's presence to Egypt and qualified him as God's instrument of deliverance. It was Moses' time on the blazing mountaintop of Sinai, encompassed in the cloud of the holy presence of the Almighty for forty days and nights, which released such revelation and wisdom that a multitude of escaped slaves were transformed into a mighty nation. It was the glory of God on Moses' face that caused the people to realize God had truly spoken to him. It was Moses' faithful pursuit of God in

> It was Moses' encounter with the burning bush that qualified him as God's instrument of deliverance.

the tent of His presence that modeled for the entire encampment the absolute importance, the life-sustaining necessity, of communion with the living God. Joshua, the servant of Moses, understood this better than anyone else. When Moses left the tent of meeting, Joshua stayed behind in God's presence.

"I believe the Lord is saying that we all need to be like Moses," I shared. "It was God's presence and communion with him that enabled him to lead Israel. It's that same intimacy with God that enables us. Without revelation, we cannot lead God's people. *'Unless the Lord builds the house,* [we] *labor in vain who build it'* (Psalm 127:1)."

Everyone listened intently, intrigued by what I was sharing. It was obvious that I had struck a chord in their hearts. I suddenly realized, as I looked around the table with genuine love for these servants of God, that each one of us had a passionate desire for God's presence. We also experienced many of the same frustrations—the ever-present demands of organization, administration, maintenance, and fund-raising, to name a few—responsibilities that often usurped our time, depleted our energy, and diverted our attention from our calling as undershepherds. In that instant the Lord opened my eyes to see the terrible dilemma that many pastors throughout the body of Christ contend with in ministry.

## A Terrible Dilemma

A picture flashed into my mind spontaneously. I saw a huge luxury cruise ship, the size of the QEII, surging through the ocean. Its massive hulk was moving forward with incredible momentum. A lone man stood on the bow with a canoe paddle. He desperately tried to change the direction of the massive vessel. He paddled with all his might, expending every ounce of his energy, but the vessel wouldn't budge from its course. All his efforts seemed futile. He was hopelessly assigned to be the captain of a vessel he was unable to steer, and his frail efforts had exhausted him. Sadly, he remained at his post, refusing to quit. He just kept on paddling.

I came undone as the Lord revealed this terrible dilemma to me. I couldn't hold back the tears. Weeping uncontrollably, I looked into the faces of my fellow pastors. "We must pray," I managed to get out, and then I shared the vision with them. "So many pastors are like men trying to turn an ocean liner with a canoe paddle. Enslaved on administrative treadmills of religious programming, their hearts are breaking because they can't get free to pursue His presence. It isn't that they don't want to; the ship they captain won't let them. They are desperately trying to get the church into the presence of God with a canoe paddle. The organizational momentum just won't yield to their efforts."

I was heartbroken by what the Lord was showing me: Weary pastors and undernourished congregations, all victims of an unbiblical definition of pastoring. God's servants were being required to accomplish an impossible task that God never called them to perform. The church has demanded that they be CEOs instead of letting them be a precious gift from God for the spiritual direction and nourishment of the flock.

We prayed together for several minutes as fellow pastors, sharing our common passion for His presence and interceding for the countless ministers longing for greater intimacy with God for themselves and their churches. We ended with a prayer of agreement: "Lord, our heart's cry is for intimacy with You. Free us, and all Your pastors, to spend time as Moses did in Your presence."

## Are You Listening?

We stood to exchange goodbyes. I quickly made my way to the door. I was halfway to the exit when a sudden unexpected tug on my arm stopped me in my tracks. "Dale, do you have a few minutes? I really need to talk to you."

I turned to respond. I instantly could see the hunger on my brother's face.

"Sure, let's step in here," I said, as I pointed to the entrance to a small chapel nearby.

"You've got to tell me more about your time with the Lord," he appealed to me, his concern evident in his voice. "What you're experiencing is the longing of my heart, but I just can't seem to hear God's voice clearly, like you described. I've tried everything. I read the Scriptures, I use devotional materials, I've studied some of the most famous authors regarding intimacy with God, but nothing's working. I'm so frustrated! I just don't know what else to do."

"Jesus promised us that we would hear His voice," I said reassuringly. "I'm convinced that God desires intimacy with us more than we could possibly want intimacy with Him. He loves to talk with His kids."

I quickly shared with him a vision that God had given me, carefully describing the hidden entrance located on the road of life that leads to the well of His presence. [3] "You have found the entrance into His presence," I said. I could see his countenance change. A glimmer of hope sparkled in his eyes as I encouraged him. "The Lord promises us that if we seek Him with all our hearts, we will find Him. (See Jeremiah 29:13.)

> The Lord promises us that if we seek Him with all our hearts, we will find Him.

"But now you must take the next step; you have left out a very important ingredient. Once you get into His presence, you must learn how to listen. God wants to speak to you. In fact, I'm certain that He is speaking to you, but you just need to recognize His voice."

## Tingling Ears

"I really need some help!" my friend exclaimed. "What am I missing here?"

Immediately, the Holy Spirit brought to my mind a passage from the Old Testament:

*Now the boy Samuel was ministering to the LORD before Eli. And word from the LORD was rare in those days, visions were infrequent. It happened at that time as Eli was lying down in his place (now his eyesight had begun to grow dim and he could not see well), and the lamp of God had not yet gone out, and Samuel was lying down in the temple of the LORD where the ark of God was, that the LORD called Samuel; and he said, "Here I am." Then he ran to Eli and said, "Here I am, for you called me." But he said, "I did not call, lie down again." So he went and lay down. The LORD called yet again, "Samuel!" So Samuel arose and went to Eli and said, "Here I am, for you called me." But he answered, "I did not call, my son, lie down again." Now Samuel did not yet know the LORD, nor had the word of the LORD yet been revealed to him. So the LORD called Samuel again for the third time. And he arose and went to Eli and said, "Here I am, for you called me." Then Eli discerned that the LORD was calling the boy. And Eli said to Samuel, "Go lie down, and it shall be if He calls you, that you shall say, 'Speak, LORD, for Your servant is listening.'" So Samuel went and lay down in his place. Then the LORD came and stood and called as at other times, "Samuel! Samuel!" And Samuel said, "Speak, for Your servant is listening." The LORD said to Samuel, "Behold, I am about to do a thing in Israel at which both ears of everyone who hears it will tingle."...Thus Samuel grew and the LORD was with him and let none of his words fail.* (1 Samuel 3:1–11, 19)

The implications of this passage burst into my understanding. Samuel was in the tabernacle of God. The golden lampstand burned brightly, illuminating the room. Samuel lay close to the ark of the covenant where God dwelled. He was in God's presence, but Samuel didn't recognize God's voice. He needed someone to help him discern what God sounds like.

Samuel's mentor was Eli, a seasoned priest. Eli was not perfect. In fact, he had some very serious flaws in his life. Still, he was available to God and an experienced listener. God chose Eli to mentor this young prophet-to-be. Before God could use Samuel as one of the most anointed prophets of the Old Testament, the young boy had to learn how to clearly discern the voice of God.

> Samuel needed someone to help him discern what God sounds like.

The Almighty had already determined Samuel's future destiny. God purposed to use him as His messenger to anoint Saul and David as kings of Israel. He was to be a chosen, powerful prophet, a spokesman for God. However, everything hinged on his ability to hear God's voice clearly. God had to teach him to see and hear through the instruction of Eli.

## The Ancient Secret Revealed

"I'm not an expert," I said. "I can only share with you what I have learned and experienced."

"Please," my fellow pastor responded, "I'm eager to know what made such a profound difference in your life."

"I have discovered that there is a simple, all-important key to hearing God's voice," I explained. "This is the secret that has opened an incredible door for me of intimacy with the Lord."

He listened with focused attention, savoring every word.

"God rarely speaks in an audible voice," I continued. "He almost always speaks to me in pictures. They flash into my mind spontaneously when I am in His presence."

I quickly opened my Bible, turning to the reliable words of an Old Testament prophet. "Listen carefully to this verse. This passage of Scripture has changed my life. This is the key!" I exclaimed with the enthusiasm of a child about to reveal a precious, secret treasure to a trusted friend.

Suddenly, as I observed the genuine desire on the face of my fellow pastor, I realized why God had insisted upon me coming to this meeting. He sent me here so that I could share this insight with someone else who longed for intimacy with Him as I did. My heart was filled with joy and excitement.

"This is the key!" I emphasized as I located the text. "If you can grasp this, it can unlock incredible intimacy with God for you. I believe that this is one of the secrets that enabled the prophets to discern God's voice."

I read the words out loud:

*I will stand at my watch and station myself on the ramparts; I will **look** to **see** what He will **say** to me....*
(Habakkuk 2:1 NIV, emphasis added)

"Do you get it?" I asked, trusting that the Holy Spirit would illuminate this simple truth to my brother in Christ. "Habakkuk, the prophet, was *watching* so that he could *hear!*

> God speaks through visions and dreams. We *see* His voice!

"In the natural, we hear with our ears, not our eyes," I explained. "But in the spiritual realm, God speaks through visions and dreams. His voice almost always comes in the form of a picture. We *see* His voice! That's why the prophets were called *seers*. They saw what God was saying."

## Open Our Spiritual Eyes, Lord

My heart was filled with thanksgiving as I made the short drive back home. "Jesus," I prayed. "Thank You so much for teaching me to hear Your voice. Lord, so many of

Your children are on a quest for You. They desperately want to hear You speak to them. Help me to be an encouragement to them, Lord. Show them the key that will open their spiritual eyes to recognize Your voice."

The thought of multitudes of pastors caught in the trap of religious activity was excruciating to me. The faces of each pastor around the meeting table that morning flashed before me. I realized how much I loved each one of them.

"Jesus, set all Your shepherds free to seek Your face," I prayed. "Release them from the prison of running their churches as businesses or being trapped in the role of fund-raisers. Call them into Your presence. Their job is to show Your people how to get to the well of Your presence. How can they do that if they are unable to reach it themselves? [4]

"How many pastors exist who need to know how to recognize Your voice clearly? I know that if they hear Your heart-cry for intimacy and respond to You, Lord, their congregations will be transformed. If they will just make time to come into the secret place, it will release Your purpose and power in them.

"There are so many of Your children who are caught up in the affairs of life that they have never heard Your voice, Lord. Open their ears and the eyes of their hearts, Jesus. Speak to them personally, intimately, in the secret place."

## God Wants to Speak to You

God wants to speak directly to you, but He speaks very softly. He told the prophet Elijah to stand on the mountain before Him. A powerful wind roared through the mountains, but the Lord was not in the wind. Then an earthquake shook the ground that Elijah stood upon. He trembled with the fear of God, but God was not in the earthquake. Then fire exploded around him, but God was not in the fire. After the fire, there came a gentle blowing. When Elijah heard it, he knew it was God's voice. (See 1 Kings 19:11–13.)

We must learn to listen. The only way to hear Him is to get close enough and then wait for Him to speak. God whispers to us most of the time. His voice comes as a slight impression in our spirits, a picture flashed upon the screen of our thoughts. He is a sight and sound God!

*I pray that the eyes of your heart may be enlightened, so that you will know what is the hope of His calling, what are the riches of the glory of His inheritance in the saints, and what is the surpassing greatness of His power toward us who believe.* (Ephesians 1:18–19)

## Keeping a Promise

I turned into my tree-lined driveway and punched the button on the garage door opener. The day was already more than half gone, but I had not forgotten my promise to the Lord. I had an appointment to keep with Him in the secret place.

David's words raced through my mind. They perfectly expressed my own passion to be in His presence:

*One thing I have asked from the LORD, that I shall seek: That I may dwell in the house of the LORD all the days of my life, to behold the beauty of the LORD and to meditate in His temple. For in the day of trouble He will conceal me in His tabernacle; in the secret place of His tent He will hide me; He will lift me up on a rock.* (Psalm 27:4–5)

Then Andrew Murray's words came to mind: "Whenever God gives a vision to a saint, He puts him, as it were, in the shadow of His hand, and the saint's duty is to be still and listen." [5]

I went into my study, closed the door, sat down in my prayer chair, opened my journal, and bowed my head. "I'm here to walk with You, Jesus. What do You want to say to me today? I'm watching...."

chapter three

# Willing to Wait

————————◆◀◆▶◆————————

Early morning sunlight glistened on the roof of the tabernacle. The wilderness camp began to stir with the gentle beginnings of a new day. It was the Sabbath.

A wonderfully familiar smell drifted across the encampment, filling the atmosphere with the enticing aroma of freshly baking bread.

"Do you smell it?" Joseph asked, as he tightened the sash around his robe.

"Oh, yes, my dear!" Salome replied. "I just love the sweet fragrance of the showbread. I couldn't wait for this morning. I've been thinking about it all night."

Salome stepped outside the tent. Drops of dew fell on her bare arm from the night's deposit on the tent flap. The cool morning desert air was like a healing balm. She breathed deeply, savoring the wonderful essence.

"The bread of His presence," she whispered with genuine reverence.

Joseph followed behind her. They stood arm in arm, looking over the tops of the tents. From their vantage point among the dwellings of the tribe of Judah, Joseph's eyes caught the slender wisp of smoke as it rose near the tabernacle. "It's almost ready," he said, gently caressing Salome's delicate shoulder. "Soon it will be time for the priests to enter the Holy Place."

"It's as if we were in His presence ourselves," Salome responded, looking up into the loving eyes of her husband.

"We are," he said in a reverential tone. "We are."

## Twelve Loaves

An entire week had passed, and now the outer court of the tabernacle bustled with activity. A heightened sense of anticipation filled the hearts of each assigned priest. They arrived early. Some had even fasted through the night in preparation for their responsibilities.

The fire was glowing with red-hot embers as they passed by the altar of sacrifice and made their way to the brazen laver. Each one washed in the pool, cleansing away any sinful defilement. [1] Dressed in their priestly garments, they stood eagerly waiting to receive the freshly baked showbread. Everything was ready. (See Leviticus 24:5–9.)

The twelve steaming loaves were carefully laid upon the tray. As each priest looked upon the loaves, the faces of his friends and neighbors passed through his mind.

"Twelve loaves," Abijah said. "One for each tribe." He reached across the tray, lovingly nudging the stack of flat bread to position it exactly in the center. The instant his hand touched the warm crusty surface of the bottom loaf, the tribe of Dan flashed before him.

*They're so faithful,* he thought. *They guard us from the enemies that seek to attack us from behind on our journey.*

Abijah bowed his head as he prayed aloud, "Thank You, God, for this faithful tribe of courageous men and women. Bless them. Let them abide in Your presence. Hear their prayers and petitions."

Lost in his own intercession, he didn't notice that the other priests were also praying. Each tribe was lifted before the Almighty as the priests identified with God's chosen people.

## Transformation

The time had arrived. The veil was drawn back to allow the priests entrance into the Holy Place; and for a few, brief moments, a ray of light from the outer court broke through the opening like an exploding flashbulb and exposed the sacred environment inside. Carrying the fresh loaves of bread, the priests quickly stepped inside. The curtain was immediately closed, leaving the outside observers with only a mental snapshot of the interior.

Abijah loved this atmosphere more than any place else on earth. "I could stay here forever," he whispered.

His fellow priests, almost in unison, softly hummed their agreement, "Hmmm, hmmm." It sounded melodious, almost like a chant of worship.

The seven oil lamps on the golden lampstand flickered gently in the air as the priests passed by, moving toward the golden-crowned rectangular table to their right. Their shadows danced on the cloth walls that surrounded them. They were enclosed in God's anteroom. [2]

A new and stronger aroma quickly overpowered the smell of the fresh bread. The scent of holy incense filled the atmosphere.

Abijah drew a deep breath and held it. Time seemed to stand still. He felt an unseen weight upon his shoulders. The atmosphere was thick with the presence of God. It was tangible, almost liquid. Every one of his senses came alive.

"Do you feel it?" he asked.

"Yes," came the reply. "Yes!" And then another, "Yes!"

"He is here!" Abijah breathed the words more than spoke them.

Carefully, so as not to drop a crumb, several priests began to systematically lift last week's twelve loaves from the table of showbread. The bread had been there for seven days, soaking in the atmosphere of the Holy Place. It now was infused with a wonderful new aroma, the sweet fragrance of the holy incense that burned on the altar just across the room. A transparent film of oil thinly covered the surface of each loaf, a pure residue deposited there by the flickering wicks of the oil lamps.

*It's been transformed*, Abijah silently acknowledged as he held a loaf in his hands. *It's not the same bread it was a week ago.* A distinct change had occurred. When it was first placed on the table, it was showbread. Each loaf represented one of the twelve tribes of the nation. *Now it is the bread of His presence,* Abijah affirmed. *It is soaked in His presence, saturated with divine oil.*

> Let us carry the aroma of Your presence and live in the power of Your anointing.

He began to pray. "Adonai, just as this bread is changed, touch Your people with Your holy presence. Transform us. Let us carry the aroma of God. Let us live in the power of Your anointing."

Abijah transferred the final loaf from the table, placing it on the metal tray. The table of showbread was now empty.

The freshly baked loaves were then lifted from their resting place and positioned on the sacred table in two rows, six loaves in each row. Then Abijah sprinkled a generous amount of pure frankincense over the assembled stacks of bread. Each priest carefully examined the tabletop. When they were fully satisfied that everything had been done properly, their nods indicated their approval. Their task was completed. The people of God would be represented before Him for another week. God would transform them in His presence. Only one thing remained to be done.

They gathered in a small circle in the dim light of the Holy Place. Abijah reached for one of the previous week's loaves. He lifted it from the tray and held it in his hands as the others waited respectfully. Abijah was the senior priest among them. They loved this man who had mentored them. He had taught them their duties, patiently enduring their novice attempts to serve God, until finally they had advanced to a place of inclusion in the tabernacle responsibilities. Their names were now regularly seen on the schedule of duties in God's house.

"This is sacred bread," Abijah said. "We are so blessed, my sons. We have the great privilege of eating it in His presence." He broke the loaf, tearing off a generous piece for each of the priests clustered in the Holy Place. One by one, each man received a portion. They ate in silence, enveloped in the sacred atmosphere. For hours they lingered in God's presence. Finally, begrudgingly, they knew it was time to go.

Abijah stepped through the veil into the bright daylight of the outer court. With a shared reluctance, his fellow priests followed. None of them wanted to leave His presence.

The remaining loaves were handed to the eagerly waiting priests and quickly delivered to Aaron for distribution among his sons. They each, in turn, would eat the bread of His presence in a holy place. [3]

## A Beautiful Morning

Abijah made his way unhurriedly along the pathway between the tents. The sounds of children at play filled the air. Laughter emanated from one tent as the family inside lingered over their morning meal. There was a restful peace over the encampment. He paused for a moment and then turned to look back over his shoulder. In his mind, he could see the Holy Place and the fresh bread on the table. He would replay this scene over and over in his thoughts until he would be allowed to step into God's presence again in seven days.

An excited voice called from up ahead, startling him back to reality. "Abijah, Abijah, good morning!"

He turned to look in the direction of the greeting. "Hello, Salome," he said lovingly. "How are you today, my daughter?"

"I couldn't be better, Father. What a beautiful morning!"

"Yes," he agreed. "It is beautiful."

"Joseph, my father is here," she called into the tent. "Come and say 'hello.'"

Joseph appeared in the doorway. "You look well, Father. You have a glow about you."

"Yes, I know," the faithful priest replied. "I have been in His presence."

Joseph stepped forward to greet his father-in-law. The two men stood in the street locked in a holy embrace. Tears filled Joseph's eyes. "I smell the bread, Dad," he said. "I smell the bread!"

When they finally dropped their arms and Joseph had wiped his cheek with his forefinger, Salome asked in a tender voice, "Can you stay for something to eat?"

"No thanks, Salome," Abijah replied. "I've just eaten."

## So That's Why!

I was deeply involved in writing this vivid scene when I was abruptly interrupted by a gentle voice coming from within my spirit. "Dale," the Holy Spirit said, "What does the showbread do?"

My eyes focused more intently on the computer screen. "I'm busy writing here, Lord."

The voice came again, this time more insistent. "Dale, what does the showbread do?"

It was useless now. *No sense trying to write any more,* I thought.

My intellect kicked into gear. "Well," I responded. "The showbread represents the Word of God. It is a symbol for the Scriptures. Just like the ancient priests ate the showbread, we are supposed to consume Your Word. It will feed us spiritually."

I was confident about my answer. All of my Christian life I had been taught by the best Bible scholars that the showbread represented God's Word. I had checked all the commentaries and read all the books.

"Dale, I don't think you heard Me!" the Holy Spirit persisted. "I asked, 'What does the showbread *do*?'"

"What does it *do*?" I repeated. I felt like the student who mistakenly answered a different question on the test than the one the teacher asked. "Well, Lord, it doesn't *do* anything," I stated. "It just sits there on the table."

> The showbread doesn't represent God's Word; it represents God's people.

"Exactly!" came the response. "It just sits there soaking in My presence. The showbread doesn't represent My Word," He continued. "It represents My people."

The revelation exploded within me.

"That's what the Father desires," the Spirit continued. "Just as the showbread sits in My presence doing nothing, I want My children to come into My presence and be saturated in the holy atmosphere of worship, prayer, and revelation. They don't need to *do* anything—just sit there!"

It all made sense now. "So that's why people are lying prostrate on the floor for hours in worship," I gasped with astonishment. "They're soaking in Your presence." The phrase "doing carpet time" really took on greater significance to me. I myself was spending hours sitting in my lounge chair with my surround-sound system cranked up loud, playing worship music. At times, I would weep as the awesome presence of God filled my family room. I had no desire to watch television anymore. Why should I waste my time when I could be enveloped in His presence?

> "I long for My people to come and simply sit at My feet."

Then I heard the Lord say, "I want My people to be saturated with My presence. I long for them to come and simply sit at My feet. I want to transform them into the living bread of My presence."

## Authentic Passion

David's words flooded into my thoughts:

*When You said, "Seek My face," my heart said to You, "Your face, O LORD, I shall seek."* (Psalm 27:8)

*As the deer pants for the water brooks, so my soul pants for You, O God. My soul thirsts for God, for the living God; when shall I come and appear before God?* (Psalm 42:1–2)

I could certainly identify with David's passion. How many hours and days he must have spent on the Judean hillsides, strumming his harp, singing, and worshipping God. In that place of intimacy, David composed the songs that all of Israel would sing in worship. He not only carried the distinct odor of the outdoors and the smell of the flock, but he was also perfumed in the spiritual aroma of God's presence. His countenance was transformed. Could this be what the prophet Samuel noticed when he singled David out from all the other sons of Jesse as the one God had chosen to be king?

No wonder David placed the ark of God's presence in a tent on the hillside and invited everyone to come and worship. Called "David's Tabernacle," it clearly expressed his desire for all of Israel. He wanted to rule over a nation who knew firsthand, as he did, the transforming power of God's presence.

David was a man after God's own heart, a man with unbridled passion for his Lord. He did not hesitate to abandon himself to God with great daring. He danced his way into Jerusalem before the ark of the covenant half-naked, clothed only by a linen ephod. His actions made a profound, unmistakable statement. He didn't care what others thought of him. He understood that there is a high cost for intimacy with God. David was willing to pay any price to experience God's presence.

> David was willing to pay any price to experience God's presence.

## Paying the Price

The casual, uninformed Christian has no concept of the true meaning of the word *passion*. We bandy it about lightly. We use it to describe deep human feelings and emotions. It has become synonymous with images of intense sexual feeling. We use the word to describe forces that act upon us, driving us, even compelling us, to abandon reason and indulge ourselves in the heated pursuit of the object of our ardent affection.

All of the above is accurate; *passion* can mean all these things. But first and foremost, the word originally meant "suffering." It is derived from the Latin word *passio* or *pati*, which means "to be acted upon, to suffer." Our adjective *patient* has its origin in the second form of this powerful word. To be patient is to bear pains or trials without complaint, to remain steadfast despite opposition or adversity, to suffer with serenity and endurance. These Latin words are closely akin to, and may be derived from, the Greek *paschein* and *pathein,* which also mean "to endure suffering or to suffer." When a variation of this Greek word was used by one of the New Testament writers, it has usually been translated as suffering. This is the word that Luke used in Acts:

> *The first account I composed, Theophilus, about all that Jesus began to do and teach, until the day when He was taken up to heaven, after He had by the Holy Spirit given orders to the apostles whom He had chosen. To these He also presented Himself alive after His suffering* ["*passion*," KJV], *by many convincing proofs, appearing to them over a period of forty days and speaking of the things concerning the kingdom of God.* (Acts 1:1–3)

> *Now when they had traveled through Amphipolis and Apollonia, they came to Thessalonica, where there was a synagogue of the Jews. And according to Paul's custom, he went to them, and for three Sabbaths reasoned with them from the Scriptures, explaining and giving evidence that the Christ had to suffer* [the same original Greek word] *and rise again from the dead, and saying, "This Jesus whom I am proclaiming to you is the Christ."* (Acts 17:1–3)

The church has historically used the word *passion* to refer to the events surrounding Jesus' trial, crucifixion, death, and burial. We call it "Passion Week."

To passionately pursue God's presence implies something much deeper than heartfelt emotion, no matter how intense. It means that we are willing to suffer to obtain an audience with God. It means that we are willing to lay our convenience, comfort, stoicism, pride, respectability, schedule, priorities, and anything else that might be required on the altar of sacrifice and put them to death.

Whatever specific personal sacrifice God may ask of each of us, there is one absolute, universal requirement that He demands from everyone who truly longs for intimacy with Him. It is very clear. The price we all must pay to obtain an audience with the Almighty is our willingness to wait before Him, to do nothing else except sit there like the showbread until He transforms us into the bread of His presence. The ancient priests understood this key to intimacy.

## I Am Yours, Lord!

Waiting on God is not meant to be some form of spiritual self-indulgence. Its purpose is to let God get possession of us. When we wait in His presence, we are saying by our actions that He is worthy of our time and attention. We are declaring that He is absolutely sufficient and that we are absolutely helpless without Him. Waiting, like worship, is not a means to an end; it is an end in itself!

> The purpose of waiting on God is to let God get possession of us.

Andrew Murray, whose words I quoted earlier, was a South African pastor of Scottish descent. He was powerfully changed by the wave of revival fervor that swept across America, England, and eventually Africa in the nineteenth century. His experience with God led him to write a significant number of wonderful devotional literary gems that have become a rich spiritual treasure for modern-day Christians throughout the world today.

Consider Andrew Murray's insightful words about the necessity of waiting on God:

> In praying, we are often occupied with ourselves, with our own needs, and with our own efforts in the

presentation of them. In waiting upon God, the first thought is of the God upon whom we wait. We enter His presence and feel we need just to be quiet, so that He, as God, can overshadow us with Himself. God longs to reveal Himself, to fill us with Himself. Waiting on God gives Him time to come to us in His own way and divine power. [4]

Three of the greatest enemies of intimacy with God are indifference, the world, and self. When we finally overcome our lethargy and get our priorities right, we must still conquer our urge to do something in God's presence. Self-effort hinders God; waiting lets God be God! Our willingness to wait in His presence is never in vain. When we wait on Him, He will do unlooked-for things.

David expressed it perfectly: *"One thing I have asked from the LORD, that I shall seek: that I may dwell in the house of the LORD all the days of my life, to behold the beauty of the LORD and to meditate in His temple"* (Psalm 27:4). David was satisfied to just sit in God's presence and bask in His beauty.

## Sit and Wait!

As I reflected on this wonderful truth, a long forgotten scene flashed into my mind:

The little boy quietly crept down the stairs into the living room. His body was snugly wrapped in his soft, fleecy pajamas. His toes pushed through the tips of the attached slippers where his mother had cut the ends off because he was growing so quickly. He stepped lightly, hoping that the last squeaking stair would not betray him.

His father sat only a few feet away in an overstuffed chair, totally engrossed in the newspaper. He hadn't noticed his son's approach until the muffled squeak of that last step gave him away at the last second. The boy didn't speak. He just sat down on the floor in front of his father's chair, folded his legs, and placed his elbows on his lap. Cradling his head in his hands, he gazed up at his father, all the while struggling to keep his tired eyes open.

The father didn't look down, choosing to ignore his son's presence. He continued to read his newspaper, seemingly oblivious to the boy's uninterrupted gaze, but the little guy didn't flinch. He sat there for the longest time, until finally his father couldn't stand it any longer. He had to respond.

"What do you want, Son?" he asked.

"I don't want anything, Daddy," came the innocent reply. "I'm just sitting here looking at you and loving you."

That's precisely what God wants from us. Don't be afraid to just sit and wait in His presence. Look at Him and behold His beauty. Tell Him that you love Him. He knows you're there, and He will never ignore you. It won't be long until He speaks. Just sit there and wait until He does. Waiting is a priceless key to intimacy with God.

> **Waiting is a priceless key to intimacy with God.**

*"My soul waits in silence for God only..."* (Psalm 62:1).

•

chapter four

# Priceless Gifts

---◆◆◆◆---

The chilling winter rain had turned to snow during the night. I awakened to gaze out the window at a beautiful etching. The glistening white of the clinging snow against the stark blackness of the tree branches created a striking visual impression. It looked as if a painter had intentionally added brush strokes to accentuate the contrast. The scene reminded me of a conversation I had with an artist friend of mine just a few days before.

"You cannot paint light," she explained, "without using dark colors. In order to show white, you must use black. It is the contrast that gives the eye the ability to see light on the canvas. Merely painting white on a white background would be senseless. You would never see it."

Little did I realize that the scene framed in my study window like a black-and-white photograph was a prophetic illustration of what the Lord was about to say to me. My journal lay open on my lap. Pen in hand, I closed my eyes momentarily and prayed.

## It's a New Season

"Lord Jesus, I'm here to walk with You again today, just like Enoch did centuries ago," I prayed. Instantly, the well of His presence flashed into my consciousness, and the Lord began to speak into my spirit.

"Son, there are still many things that I must show you. Our journey has only begun. There are secrets in My presence, but you must stay close to Me. I am watching as you record what I reveal. I am with you, Dale. Don't struggle. Your journal is a spiritual canvas. Let your words flow like colors. Paint word pictures of the things that you see in the Spirit.

"All the creativity I have put within you is for a purpose. You are just beginning to see Me release and use it. Each sentence is like a brushstroke. Even emotions are captured in the color of your words. I want you to paint and describe the things that I am teaching you so that when others read them, they will feel the same emotions and see the same things."

His words pierced me with the reality of my unworthiness. *Who am I*, I thought, *to try to capture such holy things and describe them with stumbling words and frail sentences?* Isaiah's dilemma seemed to be my very own. The scene from the Scriptures played out in my mind:

*In the year of King Uzziah's death I saw the Lord sitting on a throne, lofty and exalted, with the train of His robe filling the temple. Seraphim stood above Him, each having six wings: with two he covered his face, and with two he covered his feet, and with two he flew. And one called out to another and said, "Holy, Holy, Holy, is the LORD of hosts, The whole earth is full of His glory." And the foundations of the thresholds trembled at the voice of him who called out, while the temple was filling with smoke. Then I said, "Woe is me, for I am ruined! Because I am a man of unclean lips, and I live among a people of unclean lips; for my eyes have seen the King, the LORD of hosts." Then one of the seraphim flew to me with a burning coal in his hand, which he had taken from the altar with tongs. He touched my mouth with it and said, "Behold, this has touched your lips; and your iniquity is taken away and your sin is forgiven." Then I heard the voice of the Lord, saying, "Whom shall I send, and who will go for Us?" Then I said, "Here am I. Send me!"* (Isaiah 6:1–8)

As I reflected on the biblical text, the Lord said, "Son, this is a new season. When I commissioned Isaiah, he delivered a message that declared the terrible judgment of God upon the people, a message of spiritual blindness and deafness:

*He said, "Go, and tell this people: 'Keep on listening, but do not perceive; keep on looking, but do not understand.' Render the hearts of this people insensitive, their ears dull, and their eyes dim; otherwise they might see with their eyes, hear with their ears, understand with their hearts, and return and be healed."* (Isaiah 6:9–10)

How terrible the judgment of God is! The stark truth of this text brought soberness to my thoughts. The recognition of a far worse malady than loss of sight gripped me. *There is something much worse than being physically blind— the awful condition of having no spiritual vision,* I realized.

> Let your eyes see and your ears hear, for the Lord will come to heal you.

The Lord continued, "But now I am declaring a new message. Tell My people, 'Keep on listening; keep on looking; understand with a sensitive heart. Let your eyes see and your ears hear, for the Lord will come to heal you.'

69

"I am calling My people to intimacy with Me. I am releasing an open revelation of who I am and what My kingdom purposes are in these last days. I have always used the darkness to reveal the light. So it was in the beginning and is the same today. Light shines in the darkness, and the darkness cannot extinguish it. It only serves to make the light shine brighter.

"Now, we must be going, Son. I have some very special gifts that I must give you before I show you My kingdom. We are headed for deeper revelation. What is to come is not for spiritual infants, but for the mature. It is My kingdom that you must pursue, the unveiling of My lordship. This is why I have come. This truly is the beginning and the end. My Spirit is moving to prepare the hearts of My people so they will see and perceive it." (See John 1:5; Matthew 13:14–16; Hebrews 5:12–14; and Luke 21:31.)

## In Pursuit of His Kingdom

The Lord moved with determined intent. We departed from the well's exit [1] and headed down the roadway side by side. I took no notice of my surroundings; they seemed so insignificant in comparison to His wonderful presence. *To be with Him, to walk with Him and talk with Him—this is truly living; it is life itself,* I thought, tingling with excitement. *But what did He mean when He said, "I have some special gifts to give you before we proceed to My kingdom?" His presence alone is all I could ever want or ask for.*

> God always equips His servants with the things we need to fulfill our assignments.

God is so good. He always equips His servants with the things we need to fulfill our assignments. *Whatever it is that the Lord has for me, it must surely be needed for the journey ahead,* I concluded. *He has never failed me. And to be sure, if I have need of these gifts, His other servants will need them as well.*

## Anointed Vision

The doorway that led back into the well grew smaller behind us. I'm not sure how long we walked together in silence before He reached into the left pocket of His robe and retrieved a small object. Placing it in the open palm of His right hand, He stopped, turned to face me, and then spoke.

"This is for you, Son. You will need this," He said, reassuringly. "Because of My great love for you, I have prescribed this very precious ointment. Without it, you will be blind in a very short time. You cannot see what I have to show you unless you apply it often."

Cradled in His hand was a small glass jar. A silver lid, beautifully engraved with a delicately scrolled design, protected the contents. There were no markings on the smooth surface of the container itself. Its pure-white color reminded me of the milk glass that my mother used to display on our dining room shelf.

> The eye salve of the Holy Spirit will soften your heart and enable you to see things as they really are.

"This is for your eyes," He explained. "It is the eye salve of My Spirit. It will soften your heart and enable you to see things as they really are. It will provide discernment and reveal the true nature of the natural and spiritual world. It will help you avoid deception. Use it as often as you need it, for it can never be depleted. I have given you enough for your lifetime on earth."

The instant I touched the container, a powerful singular jolt of energy convulsed through my body. *This salve must carry a powerful anointing,* I thought. *It's already releasing something within me.*

My hands trembled with anticipation. The silver cover yielded to my grasp. Turning easily with the slightest pressure, its markings grazed my palm. I lifted the delicate cover from the jar with mixed emotions. A reverent humility befitting the reception of a gift from the King of Kings subdued my childlike excitement.

## Miraculous Ingredients

My first exposure to the eye salve was instantly refreshing. The aroma bursting from the container smelled like eucalyptus. Its exhilarating odor cleared my head. The cool, creamy ointment inside was a toothpaste-white with some sort of swirling red substance in it.

All of a sudden, the realization of what I held in my hand hit me. *These red streaks are His blood,* I realized.

The revelation struck me with full force. *Oh, to apply His blood to my eyes! I thought. I could never look through His blood and still see others as I now see them.* I knew instantly why this eye salve was so important. *I must see the world through His shed blood. It's in the eye salve, and it's so powerful that I need only a little.*

> When you see others through a pure heart, you see without prejudice or opinion.

"But what is the white substance?" I asked, not daring to take my eyes off of the miraculous contents of the jar.

"It is innocence," He said. "When you see others through a pure heart, you see without prejudice or opinion. You see as I see. You judge as I judge."

*What value could I place on such a precious ointment? It's beyond what man can afford to pay.* I looked up from the container searching for an answer without voicing the question.

He read my thoughts. "My son, you cannot obtain this ointment from any other source. Only I can provide this salve. It will heal the eyes of your heart and restore your innocence so that you can see as I do. You are right. It is priceless! But I have given it to you because I hear your heart-cry. I know your desire is to see as I see."

## You Must Apply the Ointment!

"In the coming days, My church will need this salve more than ever. Remember, I give it to those who ask of Me, but it must be applied. The way to apply it is through prayer. As you pray, the Holy Spirit will change your heart. Just as salve applied to your physical eyes can sooth and restore your vision, removing the redness and tiredness, so too your spiritual eyes will be soothed and your vision cleared as you pray.

"This eye salve has the ability to heal the painful injuries that come into your life from other people or the enemy. These spiritual wounds and emotional scars can blind you and cause you to see through the eyes of hurt and pain. This ointment will enable you to pray for others as you want them to pray for you.

"This eye salve is for My church. This ointment is needed to bring healing to My bride. She has been wounded. Her vision is impaired. I have come with much love and compassion. Oh, My son, tell My church that I will give this eye salve to those who ask for it. It is available to all My

This supernatural ointment is needed and available to the church to bring healing to her vision.

people. Tell them about its supernatural contents. It will enable them to see Me clearly.

"The church has been blinded. I want to restore the vision of My bride. My Spirit is at work to prepare her for My return. All who will take this balm and apply it to their spiritual eyes will have their vision restored."

## A Shepherd's Bag

I could only guess where the bag came from, but it was no doubt attached to my belt by Providence, waiting to receive the gifts that the Lord intended to give me. The container was fashioned of a rich blue suede with a simple leather chord stitched through the top like a drawstring. It made me think of David as a young shepherd boy. He must have had a bag similar to this one, in which he kept the essential items he needed to care for himself and the sheep entrusted to him.

*A shepherd's bag, how appropriate!* I thought. I placed the container of eye salve in the small pouch and tightened the drawstring securely. A deep sense of gratitude and love for Jesus filled my heart.

"Thank You so much, Lord. I will cherish this holy eye salve." I realized how absolutely untainted it was. There wasn't a single ingredient in it that could harm the eyes or cloud the vision. It was pure, just as He is pure.

*In the days to come, this ointment will be essential,* I thought. *Individuals, churches, and leaders desperately need this salve.* I knew that the Holy Spirit would tell me when to apply it at the very moment it was needed.

*What other gifts does He have in store for me?* I wondered, patting the suede pouch dangling from my belt. *How will they compare with this priceless ointment? Time will tell.* The glass container inside the bag brushed across my leg as we continued to walk together along the road.

After a long period of silence, I couldn't refrain from expressing my thoughts any longer. "Lord, please don't hold back. I desire to receive all that You have for me. I know that this equipment will be needed for the journey ahead."

I quickly realized the impertinence of my request. He would not withhold any good thing that I might need. (See

Psalm 34:10.) *I should know that!* I scolded myself. His smile alleviated my embarrassment. He knew my motives.

## Perceiving through His Eyes

The scene faded momentarily. The well of His presence disappeared, and I was aware again of the stark black and white contrasts outside my study window. However, the consciousness of His presence stayed with me, an inner witness confirming His nearness.

"Thank You, Lord, that You never leave me," I whispered. A lightness and joy filled my heart. The world looked so different to me now. I felt such compassion for everyone. *It must be the eye salve,* I thought. *Just to have it in my possession makes the world a better place. Prayer really does change the way you see things.*

> Prayer really does change the way you see things.

The apostle John's words scrolled through my thoughts. Many years ago, Jesus had told him about this miraculous eye salve:

*To the angel of the church in Laodicea write: The Amen, the faithful and true Witness, the Beginning of the creation of God, says this: "I know your deeds, that you are neither cold nor hot; I wish that you were cold or hot. So because you are lukewarm, and neither hot nor cold, I will spit you out of My mouth. Because you say, 'I am rich, and have become wealthy, and have need of nothing,' and you do not know that you are wretched and miserable and poor and blind and naked, I advise you to buy from Me gold refined by fire so that you may become rich, and white garments so that you may clothe yourself, and that the shame of your nakedness will not be revealed; and **eye salve to anoint your eyes** so that you may see. Those whom I love, I*

*reprove and discipline; therefore be zealous and repent. Behold, I stand at the door and knock; if anyone hears My voice and opens the door, I will come in to him and will dine with him, and he with Me. He who overcomes, I will grant to him to sit down with Me on My throne, as I also overcame and sat down with My Father on His throne. He who has an ear, let him hear what the Spirit says to the churches."*
(Revelation 3:14–22, emphasis added)

## A Letter of Recommendation

Only a few moments of reflection had passed when I sensed an overwhelming desire to return to the well. I welcomed the prompting of the Holy Spirit, yielding to His invitation. He instantly drew me into the secret place.

Absolute clarity filled the spiritual atmosphere. It reminded me of my very first visit to the well of His presence. I was immediately impressed then by the crystal-clear purity of the water. I had come much deeper into the well since that first invitation, and there was still so much more depth to explore. The Spirit drew me back to the very location I had left only moments before when Jesus had given me the priceless eye salve. Jesus was waiting for me.

"Tell Me what is on your heart."

"Lord, I'm here," I said. "I'm sorry that I left so abruptly. My thoughts drew me away from Your intimate presence. Please forgive me."

"I know what you have been doing. I understand, My son," He replied. "It's important that you process what I am showing you. Let's walk together for a while. Tell Me what is is on your heart."

"My heart is full of love for You, Master." The words poured out of me with unfeigned sincerity. "I cherish our walks together. Like Enoch, I'm so blessed and humbled to be Your friend."

"You are My friend, Dale! I know all your concerns and joys. I know your heart better than you do. My joy is to walk with you. Just as Enoch was known as a friend of God, so others will someday call you the same because they will see the joy on your face that results from intimacy with Me.

"Right now, I just want to be with you. I want you to know how much I love you. You have proven your love and devotion to Me. There isn't anything I would not do for you, nothing you need that I wouldn't provide. Even your desires delight Me. My heart's desire is to bless you.

> "I want you to know how much I love you."

"I have asked of you a hard thing, and you have obeyed Me. You have not turned away, but you have sought me with all your heart. And so, I will give Myself unreservedly to you." (See Jeremiah 29:11–13.)

## An Official Decree

"Here is My promise to you, My vow. I have written it as My official decree, and now I will place it upon your heart to be inscribed there forever."

As He spoke, the Lord pulled a regal-looking document from the pocket of His robe. The edges of the fine linen paper were tightly folded to a crisp, flawless edge. A red ribbon sealed with blue and gold wax held the official looking decree closed. When I reached forward to receive it, He gently pushed my hand aside.

"No, Son," He cautioned. "Let Me place this over your heart so you will carry it constantly within your spirit." For an instant it felt as if burning red-hot coals seared my chest as He placed the letter in my shirt pocket directly over my heart.

"I unreservedly give this to you, My son," He said, with a tenderness extended only to the closest of kin. "I am your friend. The greatest thing that I can give to you is intimacy with Me. I have thought about what will be needed for the coming journey, not only in the spirit, but also in the flesh, for I am about to launch you forth into a new and greater dimension of usefulness and influence for Me.

"I give you Myself. I extend to you My friendship. From this time on, you are to see Me as your friend.

> "Walk with Me as Enoch walked, beside Me as a friend."

"Do you remember what I said to My disciples long ago? 'I have called you servants, but now I call you friends.' So this day, I call you friend. These are not just words, but a covenant that I make with you that opens the way for greater intimacy and closeness to Me. Today I give this to you. Walk with Me as Enoch walked in olden days. Walk beside Me as a friend!" (See John 15:13–15.)

I stood motionless, overwhelmed by Jesus' words, trying to take it all in. How to comprehend the depth and height and length and width of His love for me (see Ephesians 3:18–19)—I simply could not humanly process it, let alone grasp the whole idea of it. I had always wanted, even longed, to be His friend. I realized that it was a concept, an idea, perhaps an ideal to strive for—something I hadn't yet attained, but hoped to enjoy someday. But now, in this moment, it was settled.

"I am Your friend, Jesus, here and now!" I affirmed. My words seemed so inadequate, impotent, mere childish babble. *To be called a servant of God is reward enough*, I thought, my mind struggling to comprehend this truth, *but to be invited into the inner circle of friendship is beyond asking, outside the realm of appropriate action, not mine to take. And yet, this is what He gives, not only to me, but also to everyone who seeks His face with all his heart.*

*How should I respond to such a gift? What can I possibly say? What greater invitation than this: to be a friend of God?* I realized that's exactly what it was, an invitation.

And then it all came clear. This isn't a matter of the mind; it's a matter of the heart. Only the language of the heart can adequately respond to such an invitation from the King of Kings and Lord of Lords. *I'm having a mental meltdown. This is not an issue of control or etiquette. I'm coming unglued,* I gasped like one drowning in a sea of unreachable intellectual life preservers.

And then my cerebral reactor went off-line. I let go and let God, capitulating to His love and acceptance, a surrender that went to the very core of my being. It felt as if every cell of my existence was being encrypted with a single message, a spiritual DNA, an eternal, unquenchable declaration: "I love You, Jesus!"

## His Love Is Real

John the Beloved's words came alive with new meaning and potency. "I'm the one Jesus loves!" he wrote of himself, as if Jesus loved no other. It was personal, experiential, and real within him. "I'm the one Jesus loves!" This same man took the liberty to rest his head on Jesus' breast while the other disciples looked on from a distance. No doubt he did so because He knew he was a friend of God. It was not an indiscretion; it was the response of intimate friendship. John was not boasting of a special favored place, position, or office. He was entering into the invitation given to him by the Son of God. (See John 13:23–25.)

My composure somewhat recovered, I finally spoke. "I will cherish this privilege, Lord, and never boast or take advantage of this great honor. What You grant is the desire of my heart," I hesitated, "but I'm not sure how to be Your friend. Show me, Lord, and have patience with me."

"I will do what you ask," He responded, "but I want you to know that just your being here pleases Me. I love to be with you. Come often into My presence. Please come often. Friends stay close to each other."

## Jesus' Signature

Retrieving the letter from my shirt pocket, I slid my thumb under the shiny blue and gold wax seal and broke it loose. The royal decree came open in my hands. Exposed to the light, the translucent parchment displayed clearly legible water markings. The outlines of six-winged heavenly beings were visible at each corner of the stationery.

It simply stated, "Dale, friend of God, one who walks with the Son." It was signed, "Jesus."

I suddenly realized that this decree indicated more than just His friendship. It was the certificate of my kingdom commission, the credentials I would need to have in the days ahead when I would face the enemy or demonic resistance. My identity was clearly recorded here on the letter and established in my heart. I am a friend of God!

> Friend of God, one who walks with the Son.

I could sense the demonic spirits cowering in the woods near the roadside. Threatened, they were whispering, "Oh, no! He is known of God as friend. What can we do now? We are powerless." It reminded me of the seven sons of Sceva and the demons who cried out, "Jesus we know, and Paul we know, but who are you?" (See Acts 19:11–20 NKJV.)

*This is a vital part of my spiritual equipment for the journey ahead,* I silently acknowledged, tightening my grip on the parchment. *This personal decree, written upon royal stationery and sealed by His hand, will serve me well. I am His friend, and all the demons in hell will have to acknowledge its validity.*

I placed the linen parchment back in my shirt pocket. It would be readily available whenever I might doubt or fear because of my circumstances or situation. It was His declaration of friendship for the journey of life and for all eternity.

## The Song of the Lord

It's true that music opens the soul, but what I was about to experience went far beyond anything I could imagine.

We turned together and continued to walk down the roadway, two friends on a journey of eternal significance, headed for the kingdom. At first, the soft melodious hum beside me was almost inaudible, but soon Jesus was singing with great intensity. His voice aroused a flood of emotion within my heart as I realized, *He's singing to me! This song is just for me!*

"Oh, sing, Lord!" I cried, tears of joy streaming down my face.

His love song washed over me like waves of warm water. Each refrain filled my being with the embrace of His absolute, unrestrained love. There was no symphony orchestral accompaniment, no woodwinds or strings or brass, no percussion, but the force of His song swept me into His embrace. My heart pounded, my emotions overwhelmed with the absolute purity of the music. Never, ever, have I heard such a beautiful song.

> All creation listened, enraptured as He sang.

Everything around us was hushed in silence. Not a bird or animal moved or made a sound. All creation listened, enraptured as He sang. It was such a happy song that it made me feel light and carefree. It was pure joy.

The song continued to build to a crescendo of emotional intensity. Suddenly, there was a distinct change. No longer were the words or melody audible.

*But He's still singing,* I realized, staring in wide-eyed amazement. My spirit was listening, and my physical senses were no longer needed.

With the concluding movement of a majestic symphony composed by the Creator of music Himself, the Lord had transitioned into a finale of incredible emotional intensity. Words and sound were no longer needed; they would serve only to distract and impede the power of the music flowing from within Him.

> My spirit was listening, and my physical senses were no longer needed.

It was indescribable, Spirit to spirit! Pure emotion flowed from the Lord. Not a specific emotion, but every emotion all at once. Yet somehow, I experienced no pain or sorrow or suffering in it. I was engulfed in this tidal wave of overwhelming, all-consuming love. My spirit was tuned to His song.

This must be what the poet T. S. Eliot attempted to describe when he wrote, "Music heard so deeply that it isn't heard at all, but you are the music while the music lasts." [2] I was experiencing a moment in and yet out of time, a moment between instance and ecstasy. "Jesus, You are the music!" I uttered, breathless.

The song penetrated into my being. I was overcome by it. If He continued to sing, I knew that I would burst; I simply could not contain any more. Pure love was pouring into me. I was filled beyond capacity, totally undone. It drew every emotion out of me. And then the song was complete.

There was such joy on His face. A kind of playful child-likeness emanated from Him, innocent and pure. He danced a skip-like step and walked on in front of me to kick a stone in the road just for the joy of it.

"We shall never forget this day, My friend," He said. "It is recorded forever," and then He moved off down the road, leaving me behind to savor this moment.

*What an incredible gift this is,* I thought. *It gives me such joy. And the thought that I have given Him pleasure is sheer delight.*

"I shall never forget this love song," I whispered. "It's recorded in my spirit. It is the song of my Beloved, a traveler's song for the road, sung just for me."

Then I added, "Everyone who journeys in this world as a servant of the King needs to hear Your love song."

## God Sings

God is a singer and the composer of songs. The Father sang over His Son when the angelic chorus filled the heavens at Jesus' birth. The Lord sings to His beloved. The prophet Zephaniah described this truth when he spoke on God's behalf to the children of Israel:

*Sing, O daughter of Zion! Shout, O Israel! Be glad and rejoice with all your heart, O daughter of Jeru-salem! The Lord has taken away your judgments, He has cast out your enemy. The King of Israel, the Lord, is in your midst; you shall see disaster no more. In that day it shall be said to Jerusalem: "Do not fear; Zion, let not your hands be weak. The Lord your God in your midst, The Mighty One, will save; He will rejoice over you with gladness, He will quiet you with His love, He will rejoice over you with singing."*

(Zephaniah 3:14–17 NKJV)

If you ever hear the Son of God singing to you, you will never be the same again. He is the music of life and love for all eternity. His song will sustain you in the journey.

## Angel Companions

Although two angelic companions had accompanied me from the beginning of my journey into the well of His presence, I had noticed three angels following us at a distance the entire time the Lord was giving me His gifts. These angels now felt the liberty to approach me. They showed an unusual kind of respect, as though a special honor had been bestowed upon me. The third angel, whom I had never seen before, knelt down on the roadway to tie a very small brown pouch, about the size of a coin purse, to my sandal.

I knelt down beside the angel to open the small container. It was filled with a fine substance the consistency of talcum. The powder sparkled like gold dust. It was evidently a precious substance, very costly, and considered as priceless. For an angel to give it away is an act of great generosity and symbolism.

This was much more than a gift; it was an angelic way of establishing commitment. I didn't doubt that this angel's loyalty was to God first, above all others. But the angel was indicating by this humble act that he would be faithful to serve me and fulfill his duties as the Lord had commanded him. He was making a covenant to be loyal and to stand with me. This was a token of his promise. [3]

"What is your name? I must know who you are!" I asked.

"It is not necessary that you know my name," he replied. "Someday you will know, but you should know this, that the Almighty has assigned me to you, and so I will be faithful to do all in my power to serve you well. This is my vow and promise."

The other two angels, whom I now recognized as my trusted companions from the beginning, stood next to us, witnessing this covenant. This new angel clearly held a higher rank than the first two, yet he demonstrated such humility.

The Lord had assigned these three warriors specifically to me. I could not help but wonder why three angels would be needed for this assignment, but then I recalled there are two great armies of God that join forces to accomplish His purpose, the angelic army and the army of the saints. He is the Lord of Hosts! (See Isaiah 13:4.)

The scene faded. My journal was filled with pages of revelation and conversation with the Lord. Something had transpired within my spirit during this time of intimacy with Jesus. While there was no physical evidence to prove the reality of His gifts to me, my eyes had been washed to see as He sees. I felt close to Him like a true friend. A melody played within me; there were no lyrics, just the refrain of His constant presence and love.

> A melody played within me, the refrain of His constant presence and love.

What new discoveries lay ahead? I could hardly wait to see! I closed my journal, stood up, walked over to the door of my study, and opened it. *In the world, but not of the world,* I thought, as I stepped away from the well of His presence into the affairs of life. (See 1 John 2:15–17.) I would return. He still had gifts to give that I knew I would need in the days to come.

## chapter five

# The Cup of Life

❖◆❖

The last punch of a nor'easter raced across New England, covering winter's bleakness with a deceiving cloak of white innocence.

"Another snowfall, a foot deep in places," I grumbled. "Will winter never end?"

Depressed by the dreary scene outside my study window, I struggled to escape my surroundings. I desperately needed to get into His company. "Jesus, I really need to be refreshed today. I've come to walk with You. Please draw me into Your presence!" I pleaded.

### The Vile Made Clean

The moment I felt the gentle tugging of the Holy Spirit, a garbage truck rattled and beeped at the end of the driveway, shattering my solitude. Hooded, faceless figures moved about, tossing black plastic bags into the gaping mouth of the mechanism. Its gargantuan jaws voraciously consumed the vile contents. At every home along the street, empty forest-green garbage cans were left behind, guarding the driveways like motionless sentries. Some lay fallen, their lids lying upside down, slowly disappearing under the blanket of fresh snow.

*A simple choice*, I thought, staring out the window. I felt trapped between the severe reality of the world we live in and the holy presence of God. *Do I focus on the beauty of the New England landscape covered by freshly fallen snow or on the garbage cans littering the street, a sober reminder of the debris of life, the refuse of humanity, a symbol of the impossibility of living life without despoiling it, wasting it, throwing it away?*

A Scripture verse flashed into my thoughts: *"Though your sins are as scarlet, they will be as white as snow"* (Isaiah 1:18).

"But what about the garbage cans, Lord?" I asked. "What about those places in our lives where we have accumulated the trash of living? They seem to be inevitable, a scourge upon our spirits, a dumping ground of festering wounds from wrong words and actions, sinful thoughts and habits."

More verses darted into my mind:

*If anyone sins, we have an Advocate with the Father, Jesus Christ the righteous; and He Himself is the propitiation for our sins; and not for ours only, but also for those of the whole world.* (1 John 2:1–2)

*If we confess our sins, He is faithful and righteous to forgive us our sins and to cleanse us from all unrighteousness.* (1 John 1:9)

## My Very Own Cup

At last the outside world finally faded. I found myself in His presence. We were walking together along the same road we had traveled yesterday. Jesus carried a plain white sack filled with small metal objects. They kept clanging together inside the bag. My curiosity was getting the best of me.

Finally, He stopped to reach inside the sack. He withdrew a single cup. He handled the vessel with reverence, as if it were filled with a sacred substance. Then He extended the cup toward me.

"Son," He said, the tone of His voice grave, "this cup was made just for you. Every person who enters this world will receive his own cup to drink from. This one is yours. It has been fashioned especially with you in mind. There is no other like it. Your cup contains the Father's will and purpose chosen just for you. It is fashioned by My Father's hands and is filled with His thoughts and intentions."

> Your cup is fashioned by My Father's hands and is filled with His thoughts.

At first sight, the extended cup had a plain, simple appearance. I grasped the gift with firmness. The handle was rounded; it easily accommodated all four fingers of my right hand. *Why not? I reasoned. This handle is designed by the Master Craftsman.*

The cup was seamless, fashioned from a single piece of metal with a familiar feel. *This is my cup, carefully made especially for me by the Creator of every human being,* I thought with humble gratitude for His personal attention.

I tilted it toward me with breathless anticipation, eager to look inside. Around the entire polished interior were lines of finely engraved printing. The words could be read only by rotating the cup and following the inscriptions in a descending spiral. I turned the vessel slowly, savoring each sentence. It was incredible. Memory after cherished memory burst into my mind. I was reading the chronicle of my life.

The cup contained detailed descriptions of events that had already transpired. Every section contained words describing my life's purpose and plan established by God before the foundation of the world. My parents' names were there. My brothers' names and the names of my wife and children and grandchildren were all inscribed.

The punctuation was not the familiar commas and periods we are accustomed to; instead, unknown markings appeared that seemed to identify and separate entire seasons of time. Beautiful colored lines inscribed in the metal surface separated each paragraph. Only God knew their significance. I suspected that they might have something to do with a crown or reward in heaven.

My eyes raced along the surface, taking in the supernatural chronicles of my life until, almost too quickly, I reached the present moment. I stopped, unable to continue, wondering what lay ahead in the future. There was much more written concerning things still to come.

## Look at the Beauty Inside

I lifted my gaze from the cup to look at Jesus. He had a reassuring expression of affirmation upon His face.

"My Father does all things well," He said. "Now, look inside again, at the bottom of the cup."

> "My Father does all things well."

I tilted the cup as if to drink from it. A shaft of sunlight penetrated into the sacred vessel. Instantly, a sparkling brilliance burst forth. An expertly crafted, miniature mosaic fashioned with inlaid diamond and ruby chips came into focus on the bottom. Its beauty and intricate detail were stunning. A path of diamonds led through an open doorway of brilliant rubies. Beyond this doorway, in very small, delicately carved filigree—as though seen from a great distance—was a beautiful ornate crown. The entire mosaic was inlaid upon a field of rich green emeralds. A ring of highly polished onyx stones framed the entire picture, blending it into the bottom circumference of the cup.

The beauty of this mosaic overwhelmed me. Its brilliance and details were breathtaking. *From the outside, this cup appears to be very common and plain, like so many countless others fashioned for daily use,* I thought. *But the inside is absolutely beautiful; it displays the expert craftsmanship and design of God Himself. Every life must have a similar unique expression of God's craftsmanship.*

> Every life must have a similar unique expression of God's craftsmanship.

What absolute beauty each human life contains! What awesome divine purpose every life holds! We would see it if we would just look beyond the outer surface of people to perceive the beauty inside of them.

## A Flawless Vessel

Turning toward the Lord, I saw Him lift another cup from His bag. He held it up for me to see.

"I have My own cup," He said, with a mixed expression of joy and pain. "My Father created it just for Me and gave it to Me when I came to walk this earth. It is very precious to Me. I drank from this cup every day as I submitted to My Father's will. I emptied all of its contents in obedience."

I had never seen such a beautiful vessel in my entire life. It was flawless, pure silver. It exuded perfection. Jesus tilted it forward so that I could see its interior clearly. The inscription began with a crown and ended with a crown.

Paul's words flashed through my mind:

*...Christ Jesus, who, although He existed in the form of God, did not regard equality with God a thing to be grasped, but emptied Himself, taking the form of a bond-servant, and being made in the likeness of men. Being found in appearance as a man, He humbled Himself by becoming obedient to the point of death,*

*even death on a cross. For this reason also, God highly exalted Him, and bestowed on Him the name which is above every name, so that at the name of Jesus* EVERY KNEE WILL BOW, *of those who are in heaven and on earth and under the earth.* (Philippians 2:5–10)

## A Cup of Suffering

The sides of the cup were stained with watery streaks. *The agonizing tears He cried in the Garden of Gethsemane must have left them there,* I reasoned. The awful scene replayed in my mind:

> *And He withdrew from them about a stone's throw, and He knelt down and began to pray, saying, "Father, if You are willing, remove this cup from Me; yet not My will, but Yours be done." Now an angel from heaven appeared to Him, strengthening Him. And being in agony He was praying very fervently; and His sweat became like drops of blood, falling down upon the ground.* (Luke 22:41–44)

*Mary, Joseph, Simeon, Elizabeth,* and *John the Baptist,* along with many other names, were all engraved upon the silver surface glistening in the sun. The twelve apostles appeared in bold lettering, distinguishing them from the others. Blank spaces set apart and emphasized the voice of the Father: *"This is My beloved Son, in whom I am well-pleased"* (Matthew 3:17).

The inscribed chronicle was punctuated at its conclusion with bold lettering, "It is finished!" Two elaborate keys appeared at the very end, each identified by a single word: *Death* and *Hell.*

Although He did not speak, His words resounded within me: *"Do not be afraid; I am the First and the Last. I am he who lives, and was dead, and behold, I am alive forevermore. Amen. And I have the keys of Hades and of Death"* (Revelation 1:17–18 NKJV).

## A Cup of Obedience

The bottom of His cup was pure gold, stamped like a coin. The outer circumference of this circular medallion was inscribed with the words, "Glory, Honor, Majesty, Power, and Dominion Be unto Him." In the center, the ark of the covenant was embossed, overlaid with the words, "Jesus, Name above All Names, The Fullness of the Godhead Bodily." Two cherubim stood on either side of His name. The outer edge of the medallion was a beautiful royal crown. On closer examination, I could see that this crown was composed of hundreds of very small miniature crowns, like pixels on a television screen.

> Jesus' cup serves as a constant reminder of His great sacrifice for mankind.

Jesus held the cup with great respect. He had carried it since His birth. It served as a constant reminder to all who would see it of His great sacrifice for mankind and His absolute obedience and submission to His Father. (See Mark 10:35–45.) He placed it back into the bag, and then He turned to look straight into my eyes.

## Drink from the Cup of Life

"You must guard the cup I have given to you. Keep it with you at all times!" He said with a tone of clear command. "Drink from it often. Whenever you become discouraged or experience doubt, drink from your cup. Dip it into the well of My presence. Fill it with the sweetness of the water of life that flows from My well. This is the cup of life given to you by the Father.

His words faded. I found myself standing by the well of His presence holding my cup over the crystal-clear water. *Could it be?* I pondered, staring at the surface of the well. A Scripture pulsed through my being, and then a scene from long ago and far away in a distant land unfolded in my thoughts.

An ancient well appeared, located somewhere outside of an isolated country village. It was Jacob's well. A Samaritan woman approached. Jesus sat alone, waiting, undaunted by cultural restraints, and then He spoke.

> *There came a woman of Samaria to draw water. Jesus said to her, "Give Me a drink." For His disciples had gone away into the city to buy food. Therefore the Samaritan woman said to Him, "How is it that You, being a Jew, ask me for a drink since I am a Samaritan woman?" (For Jews have no dealings with Samaritans.) Jesus answered and said to her, "If you knew the gift of God, and who it is who says to you, 'Give Me a drink,' you would have asked Him, and He would have given you living water." She said to Him, "Sir, You have nothing to draw with and the well is deep; where then do You get that living water? You are not greater than our father Jacob, are You, who gave us the well, and drank of it himself and his sons and his cattle?" Jesus answered and said to her, "Everyone who drinks of this water will thirst again; but whoever drinks of the water that I will give him shall never thirst; but the water that I will give him will become in him a well of water springing up to eternal life." The woman said to Him, "Sir, give me this water, so I will not be thirsty nor come all the way here to draw."*
> (John 4:7–15)

## His Presence Is Eternal

*Could this be the very same water that He spoke of to the Samaritan woman?* I pondered, an insatiable spiritual longing rising within me. *Yes! The living water from the well of His presence is still available to me and to all who ask for it.*

I heard the Spirit say, "This is the water that flows from Me. It is the same water of life that satisfied the woman of

Samaria long ago. It still springs forth. I am its source. This water flows from the place of intimacy with Me, here in the well of My presence. It will become a spring of living water within you, bursting forth unto everlasting life."

I could wait no longer. I thrust my cup into the crystal-clear water of the well of His presence. I lifted it, dripping with the sweetness of fresh revelation and intimacy with God. My hands trembled as I felt an overwhelming sense of being loved. *He has my life in His hands. He knows every detail. His will for me is so wonderful and fulfilling,* I sighed with total satisfaction.

Filled with overwhelming gratitude, I embraced the cup of life and gently pressed it against my lips. His life pulsed through me. Destiny and purpose, the will of God for me, assuaged my thirst. Joy and pain, fulfillment and encouragement, I tasted it all as I drank from the cup of life given to me by God. Nothing else could satisfy like this drink from His well. Identity, meaning, and purpose saturated my being. The sobering thought that I held destiny in my hands accentuated the cool feel of the metal vessel.

> Destiny and purpose, the will of God for our lives, will assuage our thirst.

I stood leaning over the pool, my thirst quenched for the moment. The reflection of the cup shimmered in the gently undulating surface of the water. Suddenly, I saw that something was written upon the bottom of my cup. The pool quieted to a calm, mirror-like finish, and the message came into focus. It said, "Dale, friend of God." I smiled with delight. My reflection smiled back at me from the pool, and right next to mine, Jesus' face glistened with an approving smile upon the surface of the water.

I placed the cup in my pouch and drew the string tightly around it, determined to guard it with diligence and use it often. I knew that the choice was mine to embrace or to reject the cup of life given to me by God. It was clear to me that only intimacy with Him could keep it full of living water.

*How many people realize what God has given them?* I thought. *Everyone receives the cup of life. What will they do with it?*

## Fulfill Your Destiny

Only when you fill the cup of your life with His presence and the flow of His Spirit can you fulfill your destiny. He is the source of life, vision, and fulfillment. Receive the cup of life He gives you. Embrace it; cherish it! Come often to the well of His presence to fill it again and again with the joy of intimacy with Him. Only He can satisfy you fully.

chapter six

# The Sword of the Lord

———————◆◆◆◆———————

A cave-like doorway led from the well of His presence onto a mountainside. The morning sun signaled the beginning of a new day. Directly across the gorge from where I stood, shafts of sunlight outlined the peaks and ridges of the mountains with glistening gold.

The view in the vision was breathtaking. I peered down upon the beautiful basin far below. Protected by two massive mountain ranges, a wide river graciously meandered across the valley floor. Verdant trees, well-tended fields, and carefully pruned orchards created a picture of peaceful perfection.

I felt a strong reluctance to leave my lofty perch and descend the steep mountainside into the valley. My three angelic companions seemed to share the same unwillingness. *Perhaps they know something I don't,* I wondered, aware that my preparation was still not complete.

"Is there something that the Lord hasn't given me yet?" I said to my angelic friends, probing for information. "Is it important for the journey ahead?" They gave no response, but closed rank, as if waiting for a higher authority to arrive.

"Lord, what is it that I sense today?" I prayed. "I would never want to go ahead of You. What am I lacking? I'm content to wait here for as long as necessary." I sat near the cave entrance beside a large boulder. "I'll wait here until You come," I resolved.

## Your Life Depends upon This Weapon

A sudden, focused burst of light overpowered the sun. Jesus swung a glistening sword in His hand through a wide arc with the ease of an expert. Blinding shafts of brilliance reflected from its silver blade and flashed across the valley through the morning sunlight. The angels immediately stood to attention as the Lord of Hosts approached. I knelt on one knee at His feet and bowed my head, trembling at His awesome, fearful presence.

> The sword of the Lord is an essential piece of your equipment.

"I have brought you an essential piece of your equipment," He said with authority. "Your success will depend upon your ability to use this weapon in the coming days. You can rely upon it; it is absolutely trustworthy."

Sensing the need for military protocol, I stood at attention and reached forward with both hands outstretched to receive the expertly crafted weapon. He placed it across my palms with the cool blade resting upon my left hand. I marveled at its lightness. Skillfully stitched red leather encircled the gold grip. Clutching the handle with my right hand, I slowly ran my fingers along the face of the blade, pausing to feel the battle insignia masterfully engraved upon the silver shaft near the hilt.

"What is this weapon?" I asked, overwhelmed by its exquisite craftsmanship.

"This is the sword of the Lord," He responded, the unflinching tone of Commander in Chief in His voice.

"But, Jesus," I uttered in denial, "this royal weapon is designed for use. This isn't some symbolic military decoration. It's lethal, designed for combat. This sword will kill and destroy!"

I stepped back and swung the weapon in a careful arc. The two-edged blade sliced through the air with razor sharp perfection. I felt so honored to hold it. *This weapon is not mine*, I thought. *It belongs to Him, not to me.*

"The sword of the Lord," I said, in hushed reverence, whipping the blade back and forth forcefully.

## The History of the Sword

*If this sword could talk*, I thought, *what tales would it tell of battles fought, enemies defeated, victories won for the King of Kings?*

With a somber tone, the Lord began to unfold the history of "The Sword."

"I created this weapon in the dawning age," He said. "I designed it to defeat all evil and everyone who rises against Me. Its first assignment was in the beginning at the entrance to the Garden.

The book of Genesis flashed into my thoughts:

*Then the LORD God said, "Behold, the man has become like one of Us, knowing good and evil; and now, he might stretch out his hand, and take also from the tree of life, and eat, and live forever"—therefore the LORD God sent him out from the garden of Eden, to cultivate the ground from which he was taken. So He drove the man out; and at the east of the garden of Eden He stationed the cherubim and the flaming sword which turned every direction to guard the way to the tree of life.* (Genesis 3:22–24)

The Lord continued His chronicle. "Do you remember what happened to Joshua?" He asked. "When I demanded his allegiance, I confronted him with the power of My sword." Again, Scriptures scrolled through my mind:

> *Now it came about when Joshua was by Jericho, that he lifted up his eyes and looked, and behold, a man was standing opposite him with his sword drawn in his hand, and Joshua went to him and said to him, "Are you for us or for our adversaries?" He said, "No; rather I indeed come now as captain of the host of the LORD." And Joshua fell on his face to the earth, and bowed down, and said to him, "What has my lord to say to his servant?" The captain of the LORD'S host said to Joshua, "Remove your sandals from your feet, for the place where you are standing is holy." And Joshua did so.* (Joshua 5:13–15)

"And don't forget Gideon," the Lord said. "It was My sword that delivered the overpowering force of the Midianites into his hands. Gideon needed only three hundred valiant warriors because he had My sword!"

I could almost hear the battle cries of the historic conflict as I rehearsed Gideon's great victory against overwhelming odds.

> *So Gideon and the hundred men who were with him came to the outpost of the camp at the beginning of the middle watch, just as they had posted the watch; and they blew the trumpets and broke the pitchers that were in their hands. Then the three companies blew the trumpets and broke the pitchers; they held the torches in their left hands and the trumpets in their right hands for blowing; and they cried, "The sword of the LORD and of Gideon!"* (Judges 7:19–20 NKJV)

## David Feared My Sword

"King David understood the strength of My might," Jesus continued, without pause. "He knew the power of My sword to guard My glory. He wisely feared My angelic hosts who wielded it. He saw one priest die by My hand. David refused to come up to Gibeon to the ark of My presence because he was afraid of My sword. (See 1 Chronicles 21:30.) Only after he learned the proper protocol did he dare to draw near to Me."

"Psalm 45 makes a lot more sense in light of this information, Lord," I responded.

*My heart overflows with a good theme; I address my verses to the King; my tongue is the pen of a ready writer. You are fairer than the sons of men; grace is poured upon Your lips; therefore God has blessed You forever. Gird Your sword on Your thigh, O Mighty One, in Your splendor and Your majesty! And in Your majesty ride on victoriously, for the cause of truth and meekness and righteousness; let Your right hand teach You awesome things. Your arrows are sharp; the peoples fall under You; Your arrows are in the heart of the King's enemies. Your throne, O God, is forever and ever; a scepter of uprightness is the scepter of Your kingdom.* (Psalm 45:1–6)

"David even sang about the power of My sword," Jesus responded.

*Let the high praises of God be in their mouth, and a two-edged sword in their hand, to execute vengeance on the nations and punishment on the peoples, to bind their kings with chains and their nobles with fetters of iron, to execute on them the judgment written; this is an honor for all His godly ones. Praise the LORD!* (Psalm 149:6–9)

"Prophets, priests, and kings feared My sword of judgment and warned of its swiftness upon all who walk in disobedience," Jesus challenged. (See Isaiah 31:8.) His words rumbled past me into the cave entrance with irrefutable authority.

"This weapon is not fashioned by mortal men. It is supernatural!" He declared. "It is a flaming fire that consumes the enemy. The angels and saints have carried this sacred blade into battle from the beginning of time. Its power will never cease; its razor edge cannot be dulled. My sword brings victory!" He shouted. My spine stiffened, and the back of my neck bristled at His battle cry.

> This weapon is a flaming fire that consumes the enemy.

## My Sword of Judgment Is Coming

"When I brought My servant John before My throne to give him the Revelation of My final plans and strategies, he saw My sword. This is how he described it:

*Then I turned to see the voice that was speaking with me. And having turned I saw seven golden lampstands; and in the middle of the lampstands I saw one like a son of man, clothed in a robe reaching to the feet, and girded across His chest with a golden sash. His head and His hair were white like white wool, like snow; and His eyes were like a flame of fire. His feet were like burnished bronze, when it has been made to glow in a furnace, and His voice was like the sound of many waters. In His right hand He held seven stars, and out of His mouth came a sharp two-edged sword; and His face was like the sun shining in its strength. When I saw Him, I fell at His feet like a dead man. And He placed His right hand on me, saying, "Do not be afraid; I am the first and the last, and the living One; and I was dead, and behold, I am alive forevermore, and I have the keys of death and of Hades."* (Revelation 1:12–18)

## A Declaration of War in the Heavenlies

"John realized that My sword is a declaration of war. He saw the heavens opened:

*And I saw heaven opened, and behold, a white horse, and He who sat on it is called Faithful and True, and in righteousness He judges and wages war. His eyes are a flame of fire, and on His head are many diadems; and He has a name written on Him which no one knows except Himself. He is clothed with a robe dipped in blood, and His name is called The Word of God. And the armies which are in heaven, clothed in fine linen, white and clean, were following Him on white horses. From His mouth comes a sharp sword, so that with it He may strike down the nations, and He will rule them with a rod of iron; and He treads the wine press of the fierce wrath of God, the Almighty. And on His robe and on His thigh He has a name written, "KING OF KINGS, AND LORD OF LORDS."* (Revelation 19:11–16)

## I Have Brought a Sword

"I will use My sword to strike down the nations when I return in judgment," Jesus declared. "It has two edges, My Word and My Spirit, that move as one to execute My judgment.

"Do you understand this? *'I did not come to bring peace but a sword. For I have come to "set a man against his father, a daughter against her mother, and a daughter-in-law against her mother-in-law"; and "a man's enemies will be those of his own household."'* (Matthew 10:34–36 NKJV). Because of this, a sword even pierced the heart of My own mother." (See Luke 2:35.)

## A Spiritual Sword

"Take this weapon and wield it by the power of My Spirit!" the Lord commanded. "This sword carries the power of My Word. It is alive and active. It is the sharpest of all swords. It can penetrate deep into the heart to reveal the hidden motives of men. Its razor edge can divide soul and spirit. When it strikes home, you can easily tell what originates in the flesh and what is the result of My Spirit. It is so accurate and precise that it can divide joints and marrow. It is sharp enough to judge the thoughts, and even the attitudes, of the heart. Nothing in all creation can hide from this sword. Everything is uncovered and laid bare by it." (See Ephesians 6:17; Hebrews 4:12.)

He continued, "You must learn to use this sword with skill and wisdom. Never use it for your own self-interest or to impose your own will and opinion upon others. Don't try to change its shape or sharpen its edges, for I have made it perfectly. It is indestructible.

"This sword has the power to accomplish its purpose. When Satan tempted Me in the wilderness, I used this sword to defeat Him. He could not stand against such a powerful weapon. Peter wielded it on the day of Pentecost. Paul used it when he preached the Gospel. My servants have used it through the centuries. It has the power to heal, deliver, and set free. It also has the power to destroy and defeat My enemies. Nothing can stand against it!

> "The Word is as powerful in your mouth as it is in My own!"

"It is as powerful in your mouth as it is in My own! It is the sword of the Lord, the Word of the living God."

## Holy Boldness

*What a great honor it is to carry this sword and to war on the Lord's behalf,* I thought, with a sense of supernatural strength surging inside.

In a single motion, with my eyes tightly closed and my hands locked onto the handle, I leapt back and raised the sword high above my head, its point piercing into the sky. Words welled up from deep within my spirit. With all the decorum I could muster, I summoned the saints and angels to attention. "A salute of allegiance to the Commander in Chief," I cried, believing that all of heaven and earth were listening.

My words thundered down from the mountaintop, reverberating through the valley below and up the far canyons. The sound shattered the peaceful scene like an army rumbling across the valley floor and blanketed the fields and river with the sound of war.

"The sword of the Lord Jesus Christ," I cried out fearlessly. "The sword of the Lord Jesus!"

The unseen doors of time swung open, and the battle cry penetrated down the corridors of history past the persecuted Christians in the Roman Coliseum and the darkened catacombs. It swirled past the Isle of Patmos and John's incredible vision. David saluted as the sound swept through his century. Gideon and his mighty men stood in allegiance to the declaration. Joshua wept in victorious praise. The sound carried back through the gate of the Garden and up into the heavenly forge, where the indestructible sword was shaped and formed in the heart of the Father. All of heaven responded. The angels joined in the battle cry, "The sword of the Lord Jesus Christ."

> The sword of the Lord is the power of God unto salvation for all who believe.

A holy boldness strengthened my resolve. "I am not ashamed of this sword, Jesus, for it is the power of God unto salvation for all who believe," I said, with determined resolve never to retreat. (See Romans 1:16.)

## He Brings the Victory

I lowered the sword and opened My eyes. He was gone.

I felt a gentle tap on my shoulder, and the ranking angel who had covenanted his loyalty to me handed me a simple leather scabbard. I placed the sword securely in its sheath and fastened the belt around my waist so I could move easily with the sword at my side.

"I can run through a troop and leap over a wall," I hummed, the words of an old chorus dancing through my thoughts. But I knew that it wouldn't be my strength or ability that brought victory; it was the sword of the Lord, God's Word and His Spirit. (See 2 Samuel 22:30; Psalm 18:29–50.)

"Lord, thank You for the honor of carrying Your sword. Help me to always seek to bring honor to You by the manner in which I use this mighty weapon. Holy Spirit, help me to be faithful to care for it and use it by Your revelation and guidance. I will serve You, Lord. By Your grace, I will serve You!"

## The Discipline of Waiting

I sat down to rest just outside the cave entrance in the warmth of the late-morning sun. My strength was spent by the emotion and power of this encounter with the Lord. I felt like a soldier who had just been issued his weapon. But even as my hand grasped the saber's handle, I sensed that there was something still missing, something I still needed for the journey ahead.

*I must wait patiently here for this last gift,* I determined inwardly.

I turned to watch the angels depart, their powerful wings carrying them beyond the sun-drenched mountains until I could no longer see them.

*Where are they going?* I wondered. Everything fell silent. The vision faded.

chapter seven

# The Master's Plans

---

I awoke to the chilling dampness of high-mountain frost and the immediate awareness that Jesus was very close. My three angelic fellow travelers huddled nearby like shadows in a dream, cloaked in a predawn cloud.

*Where have they been?* I thought, shaking the stiffness from my arms. *I'd better move around a bit,* I groaned, stumbling to my feet. I had spent the entire night on the rock-hard mountainside.

"Lord, I commit this day to You," I prayed. "Every day of service in Your kingdom is an adventure. I'm eager to see what You have for me today, what new, exciting surprises and opportunities are ahead. I want to walk with You more than anything, Lord. I love You so much."

## Limitless Creativity

I could hear footsteps approaching from within the well. The thought of Jesus' impending appearance alerted my senses. I strained to listen; it sounded as if He was carrying something. The moment He stepped from the shadow of the well entrance onto the mountainside, the large wooden chest came into view. About three feet wide, two feet high, and two feet deep, it was a rugged type of container one would expect to find on a construction site. A single clasp fastened the golden-hinged lid to the base, providing a mechanism to secure its contents.

He placed the chest on the ground and then spoke. "Today, I have something to show you," He said with obvious delight. "This chest contains the architectural plans for everything that I have created." (See Colossians 1:16.)

I was stunned by the scope of His statement. *Everything He's ever spoken into existence is recorded here?* I asked myself with childlike wonder.

"Within this chest are the plans for the entire cosmos," He continued, His eyes sparkling with the vision of creation. "The original celestial charts for the planets and stars, the locations and placements of the galaxies, they're all carefully delineated. (See Job 38.) My entire creation is drafted on these blueprints. I first conceived it in My mind before I ever spoke it into existence. (See Hebrews 1:1–3, 10; 11:3.)

"The plans and dimensions of the Garden of Eden are here as well. (See Genesis 1–2.) Each variety of tree and plant is catalogued. Every creature I brought into existence is described. I made all these things by My wisdom and power. They were conceived by My limitless creativity."

As He spoke, my mind came alive. Divine inspiration and inventiveness flooded into my imagination. In the Spirit I envisioned Him constructing the planets and hurling them into space. The joy of discovery filled my thoughts. To be there in the beginning, to see the explosion of light for the first time, to smell the fragrance of the Garden, and to hear the sounds of creatures exploring their newfound existence upon God's earth—creativity seemed to crystallize in the atmosphere.

> He is, and always will be, the Master Designer.

*And this is only the beginning,* I marveled. *God is not finished creating. He is, and always will be, the Master Designer!* [1]

## Prophetic Designs

"Some of these drawings are patterned after things in heaven," He continued. (See Hebrews 8:1–6.) "I copied these specific designs for the purpose of revealing on earth what heaven is like. I cautioned My chosen servants to construct these prophetic designs exactly as I drew them."

He pushed the chest closer to me and released the clasp on the lid. I leaned forward with anticipation. *Could this really be happening? Is He actually going to open the box and grant me the privilege of seeing these sacred plans?* My pulse pounded. I stared, wide-eyed, at the chest.

"I've always wanted to learn Your secrets and discover Your mysteries, Lord," I said, "but this is more than I can ask. To see the plans and designs of eternity—who would dare presume such an honor?"

My thoughts raced back to Enoch, who no doubt shared my feelings of unworthiness. *I wonder if he's seen these sacred documents?*

*Of course he has,* I concluded.

Without hesitation, Jesus lifted the cover, exposing the architectural drawings inside the chest. Time and eternity seemed to converge within its confines. He reached inside and carefully withdrew a single set of plans that were tightly rolled into a tubular shape.

Time and eternity seemed to converge.

## The First Ship

"These are the drawings for the ark that Noah built," He said as He unrolled them. (See Genesis 6:1–22.)

I was transported back in time as I poured over the blueprints, feverishly taking in every detail. Page after page revealed the process of construction for this incredible vessel that preserved Noah and his family, rescuing them from the total destruction of the Deluge.

The plans included an exhaustive materials list of every item required to construct the ark. There were precise measurements for each plank and board. On the last page, a three-dimensional rendering of the vessel provided specific housing assignments for each of the creatures that would inhabit the ark for 150 days. (See Genesis 7:24; 8:3.) Even a provisions list for food was included. No detail was overlooked.

"These are perfect!" I blurted out. Then I added apologetically, "Well, of course they are! You designed them."

He rolled the drawings tightly and placed them back inside the chest. *Is this the only one I'll get to see?* I wondered, looking hopefully into His face.

My heart leapt as He withdrew a second set of drawings. Unlike the first ones, these were secured with a special wax seal. Embossed on the surface of the melted amber was the outline of a heavenly creature—a seraph, I think.

## God's House

"These are the master plans that I gave to Moses on the mountain where we met together in the cloud of My glory," Jesus said. His demeanor conveyed a sense of holiness as He unrolled the blueprints with guarded caution. "This is the architectural rendering of the tabernacle of My presence," He motioned, gently brushing His hand across the surface of the cover page to uncurl it. (See Exodus 24 through 31.)

An attentive reverence swept over me, as each successive page revealed the design of the ancient tabernacle where God met with His people. The roll of drawings was very thick. Several pages were required just to catalogue the detailed materials lists. Unlike the schematics for Noah's ark, these pages included the names of every skilled worker, craftsman, and artisan who was assigned to build or make the various components of the tabernacle. Weavers, carpenters, even perfumers were listed and their specific duties described. (See Exodus 31:1–11.)

With each turn of the page, the sacred blueprints guided me through the construction process. I felt like an ancient priest making my way from the entrance of the tabernacle toward the Holy of Holies. The curtains and doorway were carefully positioned around the exterior perimeter, their weight aptly supported by the bars and posts. The smaller rectangular shape of the inner court was delineated and, within it, the cloth walls of the perfectly square Holy Place. On the last pages, the most sacred confines of the Holy of Holies were described. I could almost smell the fragrance of the incense.

"This is amazing!" I exclaimed, unable to explain the phenomenon I was experiencing. "The drawings are four-dimensional!"

*Could this be just my imagination?* I wondered. *But no, I'm looking at the designs of the Almighty. These are the actual drawings of God. His ways are not like ours. He isn't limited to the human dimension. He's the Master Designer!*

> When we are filled with the Spirit, we are not limited to this three-dimensional realm.

God created the three dimensions we are all familiar with. His divine power, moving in a greater dimension, brought this three-dimensional world into order. However, when we are filled with His Holy Spirit, we are not limited to this three-dimensional realm. [2]

The Holy Spirit added a reality beyond my human senses. He was enabling me to transcend beyond fleshly limitations into this fourth dimension, the realm of visions and dreams. For a moment, I was living in the tabernacle. He was guiding me on a spiritual tour through the successive doorways into each compartment of this sacred place, the habitation of God among men. The shadows of innumerable ancient worshippers and priests clothed in their holy vestments cast their image on the walls, as fire from the altar of sacrifice crackled and smoke rose up to heaven. The background sounds of animal sacrifices and the splashing of water from the laver filled my ears. Bronze, gold, scarlet, and purple colors surrounded me. The enticing aroma of the sacred incense aroused my sense of smell.

As I folded back each successive page, an increasing awareness of the holiness of every object weighed heavily upon me. The last section of the drawings contained a detailed description of every piece of furniture and utensil intended for use in the tabernacle. A single item filled an entire page. The first sketches detailed all the utensils, forks and spoons, shovels and pans, censers and trays. Then came the altar of sacrifice with its horns, the glistening mirrorlike brass laver, the table of showbread, the golden lampstand, the altar of incense. I hesitated as a holy fear gripped me.

I stared at the awe-inspiring blueprint of the veil depicted on the page before me. Its embroidered cherubim were fierce. *They are the guardians of His glory,* I realized, stricken by the thought of their supernatural power. Their presence sent a clear message to all who would proceed. This barrier was designed and positioned as a warning to those who might carelessly come near to God.

> **Cherubim are the guardians of God's glory.**

Even on the blueprints, what existed behind the veil was clearly set apart, sanctified unto God. To pass this barrier without permission meant certain death.

My hands trembled as I turned to the final drawing. It was brilliant crimson red with a gold border along the edges. The surface of the page was too holy to touch. It burned with His presence. In the middle of the page, the ark of the covenant radiated light. The observing angels bowed their heads in worship at the sight of the mercy seat.

"Holy," I whispered. "This is the Most Holy Place!"

"Yes," Jesus replied. "You have tasted of the experience of My high priests. Only My grace and mercy can protect those who approach My holy presence."

## All Things Are Created Twice

"Do you understand?" He asked, testing my perception. "All things are created twice. They are conceived first in the mind of the Creator and then fashioned by the hand of the craftsman. It is My creative power that brings idea to reality. Which is more holy, the idea or the substance? For without the idea there can be no substance. And without Me, there is no idea." (See Hebrews 3:1–4.)

He explained further, "It is the unseen realm that is the first reality. The realm of vision and dream, the place of origin where Word and Spirit precede substance and sense—this is the ground of My being, the creative center. This is the realm of origin and existence. This is the eternal dimension! This is the dimension from which prophetic revelation is drawn."

> The unseen realm is the first reality, the realm of origin and existence.

My mental circuits were humming. I felt connected to the power of creation itself. I could not move. Jesus lifted the drawings and cautiously rolled them shut. He carefully placed them back inside the chest in the exact location where they had rested before.

## Seeing the Unseen

*What a blessing to view these incredible blueprints!* I thought, exhilarated by what I had just seen. *It would be such a privilege to show these drawings to God's people! I'm sure that many saints don't even know they exist. If they only knew about God's master plans, they might realize the power of creation and how wonderfully His very own thoughts and hands made them. If I could only get them to see the unseen.*

Jesus sorted through the many sets of drawings in the chest, apparently searching for a specific one. I wondered what each one contained. Perhaps someday I would be able to examine every one of them. After all, I would have all eternity to do so.

Finally, He located a very large set of drawings drafted on brilliant white, flawless paper. They were tied with a royal purple ribbon. The edges of this narrow band of cloth were bordered with woven golden thread. These gilded strands hung in a fringed tassel from each end of the ribbon. He retrieved the bundle of architectural plans and turned to look at me.

## A Spiritual House

"These are the architectural drawings for My church," He declared.

I was totally caught off guard, confused by His statement. *The church isn't a physical building, but rather a spiritual edifice made with living stones,* I acknowledged. *Drawings and blueprints for a spiritual, unseen building? How can this be?* I was intrigued by the concept.

He smiled reassuringly and continued to explain. "I began the work over two thousand years ago. This is a spiritual house, and the precise details of My design are contained within these pages. Of all that My Father and I have created, this is the most beautiful.

"My Father and I have carefully laid the foundation. No other foundation is necessary."

Paul's words raced through my mind: *"For no man can lay a foundation other than the one which is laid, which is Jesus Christ"* (1 Corinthians 3:11).

"I am the Chief Cornerstone!" Jesus continued. Again, Scripture surged through my thoughts: *"The stone which the builders rejected has become the chief cornerstone"* (Mark 12:10 NKJV).

*"A stumbling stone and rock of offense,"* I recalled from the Scriptures (Romans 9:33 NKJV; see also Isaiah 8:4; 1 Peter 2:8 NKJV). You either fall on the rock or it will crush you. (See Matthew 21:44.) The Bible was coming alive as He spoke.

> The Bible was coming alive as Jesus spoke.

"My church is built upon a Rock. It will overcome every attack the enemy has devised to resist My will. My church is a victorious house, and the gates of hell cannot prevail against it!"

Matthew's words instantly came to me:

*Now when Jesus came into the district of Caesarea Philippi, He was asking His disciples, "Who do people say that the Son of Man is?" And they said, "Some say John the Baptist; and others, Elijah; but still others, Jeremiah, or one of the prophets." He said to them, "But who do you say that I am?" Simon Peter answered, "You are the Christ, the Son of the living God." And Jesus said to him, "Blessed are you, Simon Barjona, because flesh and blood did not reveal this to you, but My Father who is in heaven. I also say to you that you are Peter, and upon this rock I will build My church; and the gates of Hades will not overpower it. I will give you the keys of the kingdom of heaven; and whatever you bind on earth shall have been bound in heaven, and whatever you loose on earth shall have been loosed in heaven."* (Matthew 16:13–19)

## Deciphering the Spiritual Building Code

His hand sliding across the surface of the fine paper sounded like a whisper of breath. The purple ribbon came free, and the bundle of drawings unrolled like a majestic curtain, exposing the front cover of the supernatural blueprints. Before my eyes were markings in an alphabet that I did not recognize. The unfamiliar letters and words appeared to be a code that would unlock the contents of the blueprints. It was clear to me that no one could understand the drawings unless they understood the code.

"Lord," I asked, "what are these markings? Can I learn this supernatural language?"

"These markings are more than letters," He responded. "They are symbols. Each one identifies a spiritual insight needed to understand My design for the church and the process that is required to construct it."

His expression reflected a deep empathy. His words were charged with emotion as He continued to explain the nature of this spiritual language.

> Spiritual insight is needed to understand His designs for the church.

"Their meaning is acquired at great price," He said. "Those who understand their significance have learned it through sacrifice and suffering. This language is taught in the classroom of persecution, torture, stoning, burning, and hardships of every kind." His trembling voice revealed the incredible cost of learning such truth.

*He learned obedience through the things that He suffered,* I acknowledged. *He overcame with His absolute submission to the Father.* (See Hebrews 5:8.)

"It is not necessary for everyone to understand these plans," He said. "Their meaning is revealed to those I have chosen and given to My church as builders. They are prepared at great price. First, I shape them and form them through trial and testing. Often they must endure times of great suffering and personal pain. Only then are they spiritually qualified to touch the living stones of My house and move them into place according to My will."

Sternness resonated in His voice. "My house is built through spiritual discernment and anointing by yielded workers and spiritual craftsman. I will not allow human designs to be imposed upon My church."

## What Great Price

My mind raced across the history of the church and beyond it to the prophets and priests who laid a foundation for the coming of the Messiah. "How can the cost ever be counted?" I asked. "The blood of the martyrs, those thrown to the lions in the Roman amphitheaters or condemned to an awful death by burning at the stake, accused of heresy by a carnal leadership pursuing political interests."

The faces of those I know personally flashed before me: missionaries who died in the jungles at the hands of pagan tribes; modern-day disciples who were tortured and beaten because they dared to speak the name of Jesus or give away a Bible; believers who were cast into dank, rat-infested prisons for their faith.

"And what about those who endured the ridicule and criticism of so-called saints because they preached the uncompromising message of the Gospel?" I agonized. "They refused to cater to a crowd of spoiled people who just wanted a religious insurance policy that was comfortable and convenient. Surely they qualify too, Lord?"

## The Code Book of Symbols

The Lord reached into the pocket of His robe and drew out a small booklet. He stretched out His hand and declared, "Here, My son, this is for you. It is your codebook."

My hand clasped the small green notebook.

"For me? This is for me?" I said, realizing its priceless value. *This will give me the understanding I need to interpret the spiritual blueprints and build His church,* I thought. My hands trembled with the excitement of the realization.

"Each symbol represents a specific experience in life," He instructed. "When each test is successfully passed, I will initial your codebook and unlock the spiritual meaning of that particular symbol. This is My sign of approval to release you to work on that part of My church."

My thoughts raced ahead. *How foolish to attempt to build the church without understanding God's design! How tragic the consequences would be!* I realized. *Without this codebook, it's impossible. Each symbol represents a spiritual truth revealed through trial and testing.*

> Each symbol represents a spiritual truth revealed through trial and testing.

*What price will I have to pay to unlock the secrets of this book? Will I ever qualify to become a builder of His spiritual house?*

## A Specific Assignment

"This is your book, Son," He said in a reassuring tone. "No one else has one exactly like it. It is designed to prepare you for your specific assignment in My house.

"I appoint laborers to work on certain sections of My church to build and to establish it. Their place of labor is carefully defined, and their sphere of authority is set. Don't go beyond the boundaries I have established for you. It will only bring frustration and could even do harm to My house.

"Some of My servants have greater responsibility. They are wise master builders. They have a sphere of influence and knowledge that exceeds most of my disciples. They must have great wisdom and revelation and walk in spiritual maturity. (See 2 Corinthians 10:12–18.)

"Be careful to stay within the boundaries I have set for you, Son. Don't let pride cause you to grasp for things I have not given you to do. (See Romans 12:3–8.) There are many stages of growth and equipping that you must experience before you can become a wise master builder in My church. Learn each lesson well."

I scanned the pages of the small booklet and quickly discovered, much to my delight, that the Lord had initialed some of the symbols already. Their meaning was crystal-clear to me. Each one reminded me of a particular trial or experience I lived through. I could easily recall the lesson learned and the price it cost me.

*It's so obvious why these difficulties are necessary in my life. He's teaching me to be a builder. He's unlocking His secrets within me. I have so much more to learn,* I admitted.

## Only By His Grace

*I can only imagine what the apostle Paul's codebook must look like,* I thought. *What a price he must have paid to become a wise master builder! His spiritual education cost him his life.*

"Oh, Lord," I prayed, "My spirit is willing, but my flesh is weak. Enable me by Your grace to yield to Your teaching and instruction. Teach me Your ways and reveal Your plans to me. Let My life be a testimony of Your limitless love and endless mercy. (See Matthew 26:41.)

"Lord, not just me," I pleaded. "Grant to all Your servants willing hearts to pay the price so that Your house is built according to Your design."

Before I could finish my heartfelt prayer, a vision of a multitude of people flashed before me. They were the "living stones" that Jesus died for. They needed to be placed carefully into the church and equipped and released to fulfill their God-given assignments. Only those who were qualified and appointed could build them into the living temple properly. (See Ephesians 4:11–16.)

The realization of how desperately the church needs this ministry overwhelmed me. The spirit of intercession welled up within me. "Jesus, You're building Your church. You use people to do the work. More than ever, we need wise master builders who have paid the price to understand Your design. Please, Lord," I prayed, "send workers into the harvest."

## He Does All Things Well

The Lord started to roll up the architectural drawings. A sudden burst of wind afforded me a quick glimpse at a few exposed pages toward the back of the plans. The drawings were unintelligible to me, so new that they were still being formulated, never viewed before by human eyes.

"What you have seen are the phases of construction that are still to come," He said.

Jesus tied the drawings securely with the purple ribbon and placed them back into the chest containing all the Master Architect's designs. He closed the lid and then stood to look at the chest with the admiration of a skilled craftsman. "It is good!" He uttered with deep satisfaction.

No lock was placed in the hasp. *None is needed,* I realized. *The Holy Spirit guards these drawings. Only He can release the clasp and grant access to the plans and designs of God. Only He can grant true understanding of the spiritual symbols that release the wisdom and understanding needed to construct God's house.*

*There's a price to pay for sure,* I thought, *but it's worth every sacrifice.*

## Teamwork Required

Jesus turned toward me. "Today, I have given you the last piece of equipment you need for the journey into My kingdom. I have made my architectural plans available to you. They are perfect. You must build exactly as I direct. In the days to come, I will unlock more of the symbols in the codebook for you so that you will understand what to do. I will make plain to you, and to the others I have chosen, My design for the structure and order of My house. It is time for great growth and release in My church. I am unlocking My master plans to My spiritual builders."

A vision from a previous visit to the well of His presence flashed into my spirit. [3] Again I could see Paul as he carried the architectural drawings of the church. The apostles and prophets were working hand-in-hand to build and restore the church to God's original design and intention. Now I knew where Paul had obtained the drawings.

"Yes, what you perceive is correct," Jesus said. "My plans require the teamwork of the apostles and prophets in order to be clearly understood. I have designed them that way. All My ministries must work together in the days ahead in order to accomplish My will. The date is drawing close for the completion of the work. There is no time to delay or be territorial.

> "All My ministries must work together in the days ahead in order to accomplish My will."

You must open your heart to the other ministries so that your assignment can be completed."

## Angel Assistants

"Lord, it's impossible for me to carry this chest on the journey ahead," I murmured, wincing at the thought. "How can I walk with You and carry this large box at the same time?"

"Don't worry," He said. "The angels will carry it for you. Whenever you need to look at My drawings, they will be readily available. Look at them often. Study them so you will know My heart and perform My work well."

## Anointed Craftsmen

"You will meet others in the days ahead," He continued. "They also have access to these plans. Your heart will be knit to theirs because you have been called together to accomplish a common task.

"Build wisely, My son, for all that is built must stand the test of holy fire. If it is built according to My standards, it will remain." (See 1 Corinthians 3:11–15.)

I loosened the tie on my leather pouch and carefully placed the codebook inside next to the gifts that He had already given me. *This is a diary of my spiritual life,* I thought, letting go of the small green booklet. *One day, many years from now, those who may see and decipher this code-book will discover how merciful and good the Lord has been to me. It's my life story, the memoirs of my spiritual journey, the chronicle of my call to be a builder of His spiritual house.*

When I raised my head, He was gone. "Jesus," I cried, "anoint me to be a wise master builder and only perform work that is worthy of You. Keep me from imposing my will upon Your church. Lord, anoint all of your spiritual crafts-men to build according to Your will."

A reassuring sense of being prepared and equipped for the journey ahead settled in my spirit. *If there's anything else I need along the way,* I thought, *He will provide it.*

I glanced back toward the chest, now guarded by the angels. I had such regard for its contents. *Perhaps,* I thought, *if there's time, I may examine some of the drawings and plans. There's so much to learn and discover. But of first importance,* I promised myself, *I must learn to read and understand the blueprints for His church.*

A sudden longing for fellowship with God's prophets stirred in my spirit. *I desperately need the anointing and gifting of the prophets,* I acknowledged. *I must rely heavily upon their ministry in the coming years.*

## An Ancient Yearning

The architectural drawings rested nearby under the watchful scrutiny of the angels. My hand brushed over the leather pouch snugly secured to my waist. The eye salve, the cup of life, the codebook—each item was priceless. I realized with confidence that the letter of identity and the sword of the Lord would also serve me well in the days to come.

However, better than all these treasures, the refrain of His song came again. His voice blew upon my spirit like a gentle whisper. He was singing to me, soaking me in His love. Joy and peace drenched my soul.

> His voice blew upon my spirit like a gentle whisper.

An ancient yearning stirred within me. A primal longing sprung from deep inside; the cry of the father of faith rose up and refused to be quieted.

*By faith Abraham, when he was called, obeyed by going out to a place, which he was to receive for an inheritance; and he went out, not knowing where he was going. By faith he lived as an alien in the land of promise, as in a foreign land, dwelling in tents with Isaac and Jacob, fellow heirs of the same promise; for he was looking for the city which has foundations, whose architect and builder is God.*
(Hebrews 11:8–10)

"I am destined for the invisible city," I declared.

The angels nodded in agreement. It was an ancient affirmation they had heard before, the words of Abraham quoted again by one of his spiritual children.

I vaguely remember one of the angels covering me with a blanket as the sun set behind the mountains. I fell asleep contemplating God's plans for the church.

*Tomorrow the journey into the kingdom begins....*

# Part Two:

# Into

# the Kingdom

# chapter eight

# The Invisible Door

————◆◄◆►◆————

The light spring rain sounded like someone gently tapping on my bedroom window. Beads of moisture ran in small rivulets across my forehead, dripping onto the damp blanket. I inhaled deeply, consuming the sweetness of springtime and resurrected life. *This moist air is so refreshing after a long, dry New England winter,* I thought.

Rejuvenated by the night's rest, I rubbed my eyes with a twisting motion and lowered my hands to explore my surroundings. To my delight, I discovered that I was lying near the shore of an expansive lake.

## The Journey Begins

Startled by the sudden unexpected thud of wood striking wood, I jolted upright. "Who's there?" I called.

"I am!" came the instant reply from the pebble-strewn shoreline. "We must be on our way soon," Jesus announced. "Our journey begins!"

Ripples of water gently lapped against the small wooden vessel, a two-man rowboat. He finished positioning the oars in the gunnels and then turned to transfer some provisions into the unassuming craft.

I flung the damp blanket on the sand in a crumpled heap and stumbled from my resting place, stretching the stiffness from my body. The shore extended into the distance as far as I could see in both directions. Peering from the edge of the rocky beach, I squinted to detect any landform out across the vast body of water. There was only emptiness and the slight demarcation where gray sky met the water far away in the unknown distance.

"We're ready now," Jesus called, pointing to the boat. "We need to cross the lake during the daylight hours."

He wrestled the small craft from its rocky berth and steadied it in the shallow water. "Sit there," He said, nodding toward the back of the boat.

I swung my legs up over the side and came to rest on the back seat facing forward. The rugged, weather-beaten texture of the ash-colored wood made me aware that this vessel had made many previous journeys.

Jesus lifted Himself into the boat with youthful suppleness. Facing me, with His back toward the horizon, He grasped the oars and dipped them into the water. With a determined stroke, the shoreline gave up its hold, and the simple craft lunged ahead toward deeper water.

*Where are we heading?* I wondered silently.

I felt an uneasy guilt. *I should be rowing, not Him, but it's clearly evident that He's in charge. He has set our course.*

A gull swooped down and passed across our bow, playing in the soft wind currents of the shoreline. Another one cawed from overhead and then turned abruptly back toward the beach. Their calls seemed more like an announcement of our departure than an unintelligible birdsong.

## Focus on Me!

Jesus didn't speak but kept rowing with unabated strength for what seemed like hours. Before long, I was lost in introspection. *Is this what it was like on the Sea of Galilee?* I wondered. Visions of His first disciples flashed into my imagination. *Some of them were rugged fisherman. Familiarity with the sea is one thing, but knowing Jesus, that's another matter. Violent storms taught them to trust Him. It's been the storms in my life that have taught me the same thing. We need have no fear if He is with us!*

> We need have no fear if Jesus is with us!

I dipped my hand into the lukewarm water, piercing the surface up to my wrist and creating a miniature wake. *Peter walked on this. He really did!* I repeated, trying to convince myself. *Impossible in the natural world, but he did!*

*What kind of power can override the laws of physics? Who has the authority to reverse nature's laws and course? Only the One who created it all in the first place,* I thought, lifting my eyes from the surface of the sea to look at the Lord in admiration.

*If You say I can walk on water, Lord, I **can** walk on water. One thing is for sure, if You tell me where to let down the net, then that's where I'm going to fish.*

His voice broke the silence as if He were listening to my thoughts and waiting for my unspoken cue. "In the days ahead you must trust My guidance," He said. "You're right; as long as I am with you, you need not fear. Even though storms rage, I will allow no harm to come to you. I love you.

"But you must understand something. Because you are My servant, you will stir up storms in the spiritual realm. Don't be afraid when this happens. You are secure in My protection." (See Acts 14:1–7, 19–27.)

Jesus glanced out across the lake. "Abide in My peace," He continued. "You will ride upon the storm and sail through it without even taking water.

"Son, keep your focus on Me as we journey together from here," He cautioned. "You're charting new territory in the Spirit. I have prepared many for this final assault. It's time to take new ground, to claim My end-time purposes. It's time to possess the kingdom."

> "Keep your focus on Me as we journey together."

## Mysterious Cargo

Jesus' words prompted me to alertness. My senses kicked into overdrive, and every detail of my surroundings suddenly took on new importance. I hadn't paid much attention earlier to the two objects the Lord had deliberately placed in the boat before our departure.

A woven wicker basket sat carefully secured in the bow. Droplets of water clung to its shiny, lacquered, honey-brown exterior.

*A picnic basket,* I assumed. *No doubt it contains food and eating utensils for our journey.*

The second object, which rested beside the Lord on the center seat, looked like a saddlebag. A stiff leather flap covered the entire front of the rugged satchel. Its long, wide shoulder strap hung down in a twisted curl and lay coiled in the shallow pool of water on the floor of the boat.

*This must really be important,* I thought. *It looks like it's made to endure hard use. It must contain some sort of valuable documents. Perhaps it's a courier's bag?*

## Sacred Ground

It was late afternoon when, at last, landfall appeared on the far side of the sea. A mist rose from the shore, concealing it in a mysterious vapor. The closer we drew to land, the greater urgency I felt to stay close to Him.

"I'm with You, Lord!" I declared, aggressively attacking my apprehension by emphasizing the *You.*

The hull struck the rocky shoreline with a drumlike rattle. We jostled against the stones, bobbing in the shallow water. Just beyond us, a cloud of mist clung to the coastline like a veil, preventing us from seeing any further inland.

"We're here," Jesus said, shifting His weight with the ease of a gymnast. He half rolled, half jumped from the boat into the ankle-deep water. His plunge sent spray in every direction, including mine. I ducked, but it was too late. Water trickled down my face and dripped from my chin as He dragged the boat up onto the sand, inviting me ashore.

I gladly stumbled onto the beach and took several faltering steps in the soft granular surface, working the stiffness from my cramped legs, when suddenly I sensed that I was standing upon sacred ground.

"This is no ordinary coastline," I whispered, "no ordinary beach."

A holy hush pervaded the atmosphere. The almost imperceptible breeze seemed more like it came from the wings of angels rather than some weather occurrence.

A thick gray curtain of mist extended along the edge of the beach, no doubt serving as an impenetrable barrier. The invisible spiritual gateway obscured the entry into the interior of this sacred domain.

> This must be the boundary to the kingdom of God!

"The kingdom!" I uttered in amazement. "This must be the boundary to the kingdom of God!"

## The Halfway Point of Time

The weight of God's glory pressed me down into the sandy soil. Falling to my knees, I bowed my head.

"What's this?" I uttered in total surprise at the astounding discovery. "How can this be?" Surrounding me were footprints of every size and shape. Children, adults, men, women—masses of humanity had come here.

I frantically traced the footprints up and down the narrow strip of beach. Like chapters in the book of every life, the human impressions in the sand chronicled each individual's search for an entrance into God's kingdom. Yet, not one single set of footprints led past the narrow ribbon of beach.

*Who were these people? How many generations do they represent?* I wondered, struggling to comprehend the scene. *How many millions made it this far only to discover that they couldn't go any further because the way was not yet opened? They couldn't gain entrance no matter how hard they tried. Despite how good a life they had lived, it didn't help them.*

*This beachhead must mark the boundary between the world and the kingdom of God,* I concluded. *More than a mere place in a vision, this is a spiritual demarcation line of eternal consequences, an ending and a beginning, a barrier that only God can remove. No amount of human effort or ingenuity can open the way into the kingdom of God. No amount of pharisaical righteousness or personal sacrifice can nudge the door open.*

> No amount of human effort or ingenuity can open the way into the kingdom of God!

*How tragic,* I agonized, *to have come this far only to be denied access. To spend a lifetime searching, longing for the invisible kingdom, only to discover that it was unattainable. Moses must have felt something similar to this. He wandered for forty years in the wilderness, only to be denied entrance into the Promised Land. All he could do was look from afar.* (See Deuteronomy 34:1–7.)

The feeling of soft sand on my bent knees, the light breeze, the cool mist, the gentle lapping of water on the shore—all these impressions were surreal. I was kneeling between time and eternity.

*This is the fulcrum upon which all history is balanced,* I thought. *Right here! Right now! This is the halfway point of time. All that comes before this place is regarded as precursory. This is the doorway to eternity, the entrance to the invisible kingdom.*

## Keeping the Promise

Jesus reached for the leather bag, hesitating for a moment. A frown of apprehension betrayed His emotions. Then He grasped it firmly in His hand and lifted it from the boat. The strap, dripping with moisture, uncoiled and swung freely. The tautness of His arm and shoulder muscles revealed the considerable weight of its contents.

*No amount of paper could be that heavy. What could possibly be inside?* I wondered, surprised by the effort required to lift it. The thick, unyielding leather offered no clues. Its stiff, rawhide surface totally concealed the shape of the contents.

Jesus stood staring out toward the open water for several minutes, deep in thought. I wondered if He was looking back through time at all the individuals who had come here to this shore with hope in their hearts, only to have been turned away disappointed. With sudden determination, as though He were keeping a promise, Jesus grasped the thick leather flap and thrust it open.

The pungent smell of fresh leather burst forth into the air. The bag had been sealed since the beginning of time by the will of the Father, and now, finally, it was open! The clang of metal striking against metal rang out. Shimmering light penetrated into the open pouch and sparkled upon the shiny surfaces of the objects inside.

Jesus reached carefully into the bag, withdrew a large golden mallet, and laid it down on the sand. I was dumbfounded.

"Tools," I gasped in surprise, betraying my naiveté. "It's a tool bag!"

Jesus held the pouch open, arranging its contents, searching for a specific item. I could just barely see inside the top of the bag. It contained instruments and tools used to measure, mark, and set boundaries.

The actual purpose and function of this container fully dawned upon me. "It's a surveyor's bag!" I trumpeted with confidence, somewhat embarrassed by my previous misjudgment.

> These tools must have a specific spiritual purpose like the utensils in the tabernacle.

*These tools must have a specific, spiritual purpose,* I surmised. *They're like the utensils in the tabernacle: they're fashioned for a holy purpose and have a sacred function.*

## The First Marker

Jesus grasped the sought-for object and withdrew it from the shadowy interior of the pouch. A solid gold surveyor's pin of priceless worth burst into view. The dazzling splendor of the slender rectangular object overwhelmed me. I stood gazing in wide-eyed astonishment, overcome by its beauty. It was flawlessly designed, exquisitely perfect.

"Surveyor's pins!" I exclaimed incredulously. "Surveyor's stakes to mark the boundaries and dimensions of the kingdom of God."

I squinted in the late afternoon light, eager to get a clear glimpse of the three similar objects still concealed in the leather bag, but with little success. All I could discern was that they were all approximately the same length as the one that Jesus now held in front of me and that each of them appeared to have a unique shape.

## The Flesh Stone

My attention was riveted upon the golden treasure in Jesus' hands. Its breathtaking beauty captivated me. Unlike the plain metal stakes customarily used by surveyors, this particular pin was fashioned by God for a divine purpose. On each of the four sides, near the top of the pin, an exquisite jewel embellished the gold surface. [1]

Jesus positioned the pin in His hands, pausing to examine the first side. Clearly visible on the polished gold face was a black oval-shaped onyx, about an inch wide and two inches long, glistening in the late afternoon light. Its opaque surface, like a highly polished mirror, replicated every image in shadowy darkness.

The surface of the gemstone captured my reflection as Jesus moved the pin slightly. My face appeared upon the glassine surface, enshrouded in blackness. An overwhelming sense of guilt and conviction flooded my heart as I stared in dismay. A cold foreboding clutched at my emotions. My hands felt clammy. Life seemed to drain out of my body. I felt hopelessly lost, enslaved in the depravity of my fleshly image. (See Exodus 28:9–14, 20.)

The dark gemstone possessed a distinct spiritual quality. It was revealing something to me symbolically. The Holy Spirit's convicting presence was unmistakable. I was powerless to evade His probing presence. I uttered a groan of relief, as though I had been released from a prison cell, when Jesus finally turned the pin to expose its next face.

## The Love Stone

A ruby of immense value graced the second surface. Its expertly cut facets shimmered like burning hot coals, sending steady, radiant beams of light forth like a beacon. The warm, fiery glow reflected in Jesus' eyes and drew me with beckoning power. This marquis-shaped gemstone seemed to possess a life of its own, an irresistible allure.

"This is no ordinary ruby!" I exclaimed, enticed by its magnetism.

My mind chronicled the role of the ruby in Scripture. God chose the ruby as the specific gemstone to represent the tribe of Judah. They were known among the tribes of Israel for their unabashed praise of Yahweh. The ruby was the first stone set in Aaron's breastplate to commemorate Judah before God when the high priest entered into His presence in the Holy of Holies. (See Exodus 28:15–30; 39:8–21.)

The Bible uses rubies to symbolize wisdom and virtue. Solomon, one of the wealthiest and wisest men who ever lived, wrote, *"For wisdom is more precious that rubies"* (Proverbs 8:11 NIV) and, *"Who can find a virtuous woman? for her price is far above rubies"* (Proverbs 31:10 KJV).

The ancient Hebrews believed that rubies were the most precious of the twelve gems God created when He made all things. Even today, rubies are one of the most valuable of gemstones, rivaled only by rare diamonds. [2]

*But this ruby! It's the absolute finest in all of creation,* I admitted. *God chose this particular stone to grace the first surveyor's pin. What could it mean? It's evident that Jesus considers it priceless, worthy of the ultimate sacrifice.*

> The incomparable ruby conveyed passion and power.

The incomparable red stone conveyed passion and power. No authority or force could possibly extinguish its brilliance or weaken its supremacy. Like a fiery-hot coal, it burned with uncontaminated strength.

*Somehow this stone is bound to the first one,* I surmised. *The onyx and the ruby are intentionally, inseparably positioned next to each other.*

## The Touchstone

The third face of the surveyor's pin displayed a breathtaking iridescent-blue sapphire sparkling upon its golden setting. Refracted light flashed forth from it with laser-like precision, skipping across the water at dazzling speed. Like piercing shards of glass, each brilliant shaft cut the yielding surface with cold, scalpel-like accuracy.

I reached out to touch its razor sharp facets, instantly overcome with an insatiable covetousness for this incredible shimmering treasure. Its crystalline clarity and icy coldness captivated me. It was at once sobering and revealing. Like timeless currency, long after man's coinage has failed, this jewel would continue to glisten with sparkling purity and limitless value.

*This is eternal wealth,* I thought, coveting the treasure. *In times of uncertainty, this gemstone, portable and paperless, will remain unfaltering in its value.* [3]

This is eternal wealth, unfaltering in value.

I ached to touch it, to possess it, but dared not, quickly withdrawing my hand. Despite its magnificence, there remained an inexplicable coldness to this gemstone. Like the razor edge of a finely sharpened sword, it was emotionless and cutting. Its cold, calculating clarity sobered me. (See Exodus 28:18; 39:11.)

"Pure, absolutely pure!" I declared, gazing at it as if I were peering through a jeweler's lens.

A final ray of light burst from the blue sapphire, and then it disappeared as Jesus turned the surveyor's pin to the fourth surface. The weight of the golden stake made His forearm flex.

## The Life Stone

The opulent emerald spanning the entire width of the side of the pin cast a green glow over the golden surface. The multifaceted antiquity appeared to be as old as civilization itself. Fashioned deep within the earth, its cool, refreshing appearance had an immediate calming effect upon my thoughts and emotions.

*Emeralds are among the first gemstones valued by man,* I thought. *Some people even regard them as magic. So that's where "romancing the stone" originated?* I chuckled. *Probably just an unconscious response to the restful color. But this stone is different. It seems to carry a power that began long before man existed. I can feel life radiating from it!*

My thoughts carried me back to the ancient civilization of Egypt. Almost two thousand years before Cleopatra, the Egyptians mined emeralds in the harsh, inhospitable desert hills east of Luxor. There, between the Red Sea and the sacred Nile River, the precious stones were quarried. Cleopatra's Mines, as they are now known, unearthed gemstones worthy of a queen. But none could compare to this stone, chosen to represent the King of Kings. [4]

The sacred breastplate of the high priest flashed into my mind again. God instructed, *"The first row shall be a row of ruby, topaz and emerald"* (Exodus 28:17).

*What will heaven be like?* I wondered, gazing in awe at the wonderful deep-green emerald. *The foundations of the walls of the New Jerusalem are adorned with all manner of precious stones.*

I struggled to imagine the beauty of God's eternal city described in Revelation:

> *Then one of the seven angels who had the seven bowls full of the seven last plagues came and spoke with me, saying, "Come here, I will show you the bride, the wife of the Lamb." And he carried me away in the Spirit to a great and high mountain, and showed me the holy city, Jerusalem, coming down out of heaven from God, having the glory of God. Her brilliance was like a very costly stone, as a stone of crystal-clear jasper. It had a great and high wall, with twelve gates, and at the gates twelve angels; and names were written on them, which are the names of the twelve tribes of the sons of Israel.*

*There were three gates on the east and three gates on the north and three gates on the south and three gates on the west. And the wall of the city had twelve foundation stones, and on them were the twelve names of the twelve apostles of the Lamb. The one who spoke with me had a gold measuring rod to measure the city, and its gates and its wall. The city is laid out as a square, and its length is as great as the width; and he measured the city with the rod, fifteen hundred miles; its length and width and height are equal. And he measured its wall, seventy-two yards, according to human measurements, which are also angelic measurements. The material of the wall was jasper; and the city was pure gold, like clear glass. The foundation stones of the city wall were adorned with every kind of precious stone. The first foundation stone was jasper; the second, sapphire; the third, chalcedony; the fourth, emerald; the fifth, sardonyx; the sixth, sardius; the seventh, chrysolite; the eighth, beryl; the ninth, topaz; the tenth, chrysoprase; the eleventh, jacinth; the twelfth, amethyst. And the twelve gates were twelve pearls; each one of the gates was a single pearl. And the street of the city was pure gold, like transparent glass.* (Revelation 21:9–21)

"Mind-boggling, unparalleled beauty! No earthly city could ever claim such splendor and magnificence," I declared. "Just one side of the city stretches for fourteen hundred miles. The walls are two hundred feet high." The sound of my voice startled me. I was lost in the luxury of the incredible emerald in Jesus' hands.

> Imagine the overwhelming beauty of the holy city!

*I can just imagine the overwhelming beauty of the holy city,* I thought. God's bride, the New Jerusalem, bedecked with innumerable gemstones, sparkling and blazing with glory. The ecstasy of this single, glistening emerald before my very eyes would be multiplied millions of times.

*But who will see it?* I wondered, painfully tearing my gaze from the green glow of the emerald to look upon Jesus' face.

"Who will see it, Lord?" I whispered to Him. "Something this beautiful must be seen!"

He looked at me with overwhelming grace and understanding. I knew He was about to reveal the answer.

## What Great Price!

Jesus stood erect, totally focused upon the task at hand. Furrows of flesh spread across His forehead in a despairing frown. A hushed silence filled the atmosphere, so deep and profound that the unseen forces of the cosmos were concentrated on this very moment. Even the waves ceased. All creation was put on pause.

For what seemed like an eternity, a great struggle reflected in His eyes. A fierce battle of infinite consequence raged within His spirit. I wanted to encourage and comfort Him, to offer my help, to do something to assuage the terrible pain so unmistakably visible. But I was helpless, frozen to the spot where I stood.

> A fierce battle of infinite consequence raged within His spirit.

Finally, total surrender came. The frown of torment faded from His face and rest fell over Him like a blanket of comfort. But strangely, He did not display the demeanor of a conquered adversary. Instead, His expression revealed an absolute, determined resolve. I suddenly realized that whatever had transpired, He was not defeated. He had chosen to yield.

Jesus turned quickly and surveyed the place where we were standing. Great tears formed and began to fall down His cheeks.

"What great price, Father!" He uttered as He searched the ground. His words filled the silence like nails driven by the force of a sledgehammer. He spoke with such anguish.

Again the words came from deep within His soul, "What great price!"

And then the silence returned like a grave cloth, deeper and more stifling. In that instant, heaven wept in sorrow, and hell laughed in scorn.

Quickly searching the beach, Jesus stepped a few paces beyond the last trace of human footprints. Kneeling down, He scraped the uneven surface with His hand, smoothing a spot on the ground. Then He lifted His head and looked directly at me.

### Drive the Stake Here!

"Son, bring the golden hammer, and drive the surveyor's stake into the soil right here, right at this very spot!"

"But, Lord," I protested, "I'm not worthy to do this!" The very thought of striking the exquisite surveyor's stake was reprehensible. A sickening dread filled my heart. My stomach tightened in a convulsive shudder, and I recoiled, taking a full step backward.

"Who am I, Lord?" I pleaded. "I am mere flesh. I'm full of sinful things. O God, I will not do this!"

His reply was swift and condemning: "You have already done it!"

His words crashed into my spirit with the finality of a prison door slamming shut, forever locked. My heart broke.

> The hand of God and the hand of man have set this first stake.

"The hand of God and the hand of man have set this first surveyor's stake," He continued. "You must do this on behalf of all flesh."

Suddenly, the stark realization burst into my heart. "This is the place of Your cross!" I groaned in horror.

I grasped the hammer in my hands. It was so heavy that it required all of my strength just to lift it. A tempest of emotion surged over me as I raised the hammer above my head and prepared to strike a powerful blow upon the surveyor's pin. A sickening wave of disgust convulsed in my stomach. *This must be how the Roman soldier felt,* I choked, *when he drove the nails into Jesus' flesh.*

Jesus held the pin firmly with both hands, carefully positioning it so that the onyx stone faced toward the sea. His eyes never strayed from the surveyor's stake. He grasped it as though He held His destiny in His hands—and then He waited.

I swung the golden hammer down upon the stake with all the strength I could summon. The mallet flashed through its arc and struck the head of the pin with incredible force. A sickening thud, more like a fist hitting human flesh than metal striking metal, resounded up and down the beach.

The moment that the hammer struck the golden pin, Jesus let out a deafening cry. *"Eloi! Eloi!"* He shouted, with the terrifying abandonment of an orphaned son. (See Mark 15:34; Matthew 27:32–56.)

The surveyor's pin sank into the soil and stopped abruptly at a line inscribed into the surface of the pin about midway. The stake was buried exactly to the depth of this delineation as though a predetermined, unseen barrier would not permit it to go any further.

## The Capstone

My hands trembled as I hoisted the hammer from the surface of the pin. My mouth fell open in utter amazement. A dramatic change had taken place on the top of the surveyor's stake. Before I struck it, it was smooth, flat gold.

Now, sitting on the summit of the pin was the largest diamond I've ever seen. Its brilliance was beyond description. Light burst from it in every direction, filling the air with a dazzling rainbow of color. Perfectly cut facets released and magnified its purity.[5]

"The most priceless of all," I uttered in surprised wonder, realizing that the world-famous Hope Diamond paled in comparison to this exquisite shimmering jewel. An unexpected sense of completion surprised my soul.

*How appropriate,* I thought, *that God would choose this flawless diamond as the capstone of the first surveyor's pin!*

There are two great forces required to make a diamond, heat and pressure. From a single element, carbon, the forces of nature create unbelievable beauty. In a similar way, Jesus became flesh and walked among us. The heat and pressure of trial and temptation served to reveal the innocent, sinless beauty of the Son of God. The final blow, His crucifixion, was the capstone of His submission and obedience to the Father.

> The heat and pressure of trial and temptation served to reveal the sinless beauty of the Son of God.

The Lord stepped back to view the first surveyor's pin marking the boundary of the kingdom of God. "It is well set," He said. "It can never be moved. No hand of man can ever displace it, and no one can pass this way into My domain unless they pass by this marker."

"This is where it begins," He declared. *"I am the way, the truth, and the life. No one comes to the Father but through Me"* (John 14:6 NKJV).

## It Is Finished

I stared at the glistening, bejeweled surveyor's stake, sitting upright, firmly driven into the soil, sparkling in the

143

late afternoon light. Its location was clearly visible to all who might approach this shore. I knew in the Spirit that it had been placed here thousands of years ago, fixed forever in time, when Jesus was crucified on Calvary's cross. The will of the Father and the hands of men drove it in place.

*This is the first surveyor's pin, the entrance to the kingdom of God,* I affirmed. *All of history is distilled into this single climactic moment. Here, on this beachhead of time, a solitary stake, like a spiritual exclamation point, delineates God's kingdom from every other.*

## We Are All Guilty

I had symbolically reenacted the events of the Crucifixion in the Spirit. The awful reality that I, along with all of mankind, had driven the stake into the ground was undeniable.

"The Roman soldiers weren't the only ones who crucified Him," I groaned. "I have done it. We all have done it."

No longer could I view history with puritanical detachment. I was a partner in the events of His passion. "I'm guilty; all mankind is. Our sins crucified Him," I confessed.

> The Roman soldiers weren't the only ones who crucified Him—we all have.

"This is more than a vision," I uttered in reverence. "This is fact! This is where it commences. Your rule and reign, Your kingdom for all eternity past and future, is clearly established at this spot. Here is where the Holy Spirit draws all flesh. This is the entrance to the kingdom of God."

## The Meaning of the Stones

"Lord," I asked, basking in the truth of this revelation, "please explain these jewels to me."

"These stones signify the nature of My kingdom," He clarified. "They are symbols of spiritual truth, in a setting of pure gold, the royal metal that has always signified kingship. (See 1 Kings 10:1–23.)

"The onyx represents the flesh. It faces the world to continually remind mankind that they are imprisoned in the shadow of darkness. Every person has sinned and fallen short of My glory. All who approach My kingdom must confess their sin. That is why this stone faces outward toward the water. It must be encountered first. It is the stone of admission. (See Romans 3:23; 1 John 1:5–10.)

"No one can pass this stake without My purifying grace. No one can enter the kingdom unless he is first made righteous!" Jesus declared. (See Romans 3:21–26; 2 Corinthians 5:21.)

"Once you acknowledge your true nature reflected in the onyx stone, you may approach the kingdom. The only way is to pass by the ruby and the emerald. The ruby represents My blood. It is the only thing that can cleanse you from sin. No one can pass this way without passing through My blood. It is the only way into My kingdom. This is the mercy stone," He said, pointing to the crimson gem. (See Hebrews 9:22; Revelation 1:5.)

> No one can enter the kingdom unless he is first made righteous.

"On the opposite side is the emerald. When you pass this marker, you move from death into life. You are set free from sin *and* death. Because I live, you will live also. My resurrection imparts eternal life. You will never die; you have the privilege of living with Me forever. This is the life stone. (See John 11:25–26; 14:19.)

"The final jewel is the sapphire; this is the judgment stone," He explained. "Once you pass this boundary you are no longer judged with the world. You are judged as My servant. You will be held accountable for the stewardship of your gifts and talents. I judge the living and the dead. I judge the lost and the redeemed. I am judgment. Those who receive My lordship are judged as sons and daughters." (See Deuteronomy 1:17; Psalm 58:11; and 2 Timothy 4:8.)

"The diamond, Lord?" I asked.

"It represents My absolute perfection," He responded. "When I died upon the cross, all the sin and disease of mankind came upon Me. I became all these things. My Father had to look away in that agonizing moment. But when it was finished, My Father saw only a pure, flawless, perfect sacrifice. (See Isaiah 53; Hebrews 10:19–22.)

"No one can pass into My kingdom without acknowledging that I am the only begotten Son of God. I am holy and righteous altogether. Even though I am the stone that the religious leaders rejected, I am the most precious and valuable of all stones. I am the light of the world, and I reflect the light of heaven on earth. He who sees Me, sees My Father. My light shines in the darkness, and no one can extinguish it!" (See John 1.)

## Is This a Dream?

*Is this a vision or is it reality?* I wondered, feeling like C. S. Lewis's Ransom in *Perelandra*: "At Ransom's waking something happened to him which perhaps never happens to a man until he is out of his own world: he saw reality, and thought it was a dream." [6]

I knelt beside the surveyor's pin, embracing the powerful significance of its message, cherishing every detail, and each priceless gemstone. "It's so powerfully clear!" I confessed.

## The Threshold of Faith

"Here is where My kingdom begins," Jesus said with a finality that punctuated time itself. "This is the invisible doorway. All who enter must cross this threshold by faith in Me. I am the entrance to the kingdom." Suddenly, it was obvious to me why no footprints led beyond the beach into the kingdom. Only faith in the finished work of Jesus can open the doorway.

We silently withdrew from the surveyor's pin back toward the boat. He lifted the wicker basket from the bow, shook the beads of water from its surface, and set it down on the beach. Long shadows signaled the approach of night as he opened the lid and lifted a small linen cloth, spreading it on the ground. A loaf of bread and some wine were placed on the cloth, and then He reached inside the basket again to retrieve a scroll. Beckoning me to sit beside Him on the shore, He opened the parchment.

"Look," He said, pointing to the text. "Let Me show you how often I taught about My kingdom." He turned to several references regarding the first surveyor's stake, reading aloud and commenting on each one.

"I spent My last days on earth teaching about the kingdom of God," He said. (See Acts 1:3.) "This has always been My Father's ultimate intention."

> Jesus spent His last days on earth teaching about the kingdom of God.

We sat together at the boundary of the kingdom, reading and talking, until the day finally surrendered its last rays of light and we could no longer see the words.

The stars were glistening brightly overhead when He finally stood and walked back toward the surveyor's pin. Retrieving the golden hammer, He put it back in the leather bag and secured the strap over His shoulder.

*I wonder what the other surveyor's pins are for?* I thought. *Where will they be placed?*

## The Air Is Clear!

"You need to rest now. Tomorrow we will enter the kingdom." He said. "There is so much for you to learn. I am releasing this revelation regarding the structure and government of My kingdom to many of My servants."

*The drawings,* I remembered. *I must consult the architectural drawings of the kingdom of God. Perhaps tomorrow I'll have a chance.*

I lay upon the soft, sandy beach in the damp air, tired from the day's journey. *So this is where it begins,* I thought with a sigh of contentment.

> A distinct change had occurred in the atmosphere— the air was clear.

And then I noticed that a distinct change had occurred in the atmosphere. The mist that had veiled this shoreline when I arrived was gone. The atmosphere was clear.

*Tomorrow in the daylight I'll be able to see the kingdom,* I realized, smiling with a surge of excitement.

I could hear singing, a soft beautiful sound that came from beyond the shore somewhere within the kingdom. And then sleep brought silence.

chapter nine

# The Narrow Pathway

———————◆◆◆◆————————

W ater lazily lapped against the shoreline. Soft, shuf-
fling footsteps and the unmistakable squeak of
moving hinges indicated a holy presence nearby.
I turned to discover my three angelic companions standing
beside the open wooden chest.

*I can't be dreaming. This has got to be more than just
my imagination. I feel so alive.* Thoughts of God's kingdom
began to filter into my consciousness.

## Study Time

The architectural documents were still contained safely
inside the mobile archive. On the top of the stack, the supernatural drawings for the church were most visible, clearly
distinguished by the purple and gold ribbon.

"The Master's plans!" I said with eager delight, recalling
my intentions from the night before. "You've brought them
for me to examine. Thank you so much." I smiled in appre-
ciation as I lifted the large bundle of architectural drawings
from the chest. The closest angel nodded in response, but no
words were spoken. None were necessary. They were simply
carrying out orders.

## A Moment of Confusion

"Wait a minute," I blurted out in confusion. "I need the plans for the kingdom of God. These are the drawings for the church. They're...they're the wrong ones," I stuttered, perplexed by my dilemma.

I frantically searched through the remaining drawings, but to no avail. There were none for the kingdom! "There's got to be an explanation for this mistake," I stammered. [1]

The Holy Spirit immediately responded, breathing into my spirit a simple clue. *Perhaps the kingdom can be understood only through the design of the church.*

> The kingdom can be understood only through the design of the church.

"Of course," I said, my tension subsiding. "The church must be the kingdom made visible. I can discern the kingdom by looking at God's design for His church. [2]

"Now I understand," I said, glancing at one of the celestial sentries guarding the chest. "God's kingdom and His church are inextricably bound together. In order to understand the nature and construction of the kingdom, I must discern the church. The kingdom can be truly understood only in that context." [3]

I slid the royal ribbon from the bundle in excited haste and let it fall. My pulse pounded as I knelt to unroll the drawings on the ground. I carefully lifted the cover. To my utter astonishment, there on the first page of the Master's plans for the church was an exact rendering of the first surveyor's pin.

## God's Insignia

My eyes rapidly scanned the drawing, consuming the totality of its magnificence. Vivid colors leapt from the paper, sparkling like the actual jewels they portrayed. The smallest details were carefully depicted on the schematic. Precise measurements were given for the size of the surveyor's pin and the type and placement of each gemstone. The location of the line identifying the depth to which it should be driven was clearly delineated on the surface of the metal shaft. A notation read, "Marked for all to see who pass by this entrance."

The artistic rendering of the diamond sparkled on the page. Unlike a normal surveyor's stake, which bears an unassuming, perfunctory cap used to identify the location, date, and name of the surveyor, this pin was certified with the most costly of gems.

*Men would never use such a valuable possession just to stake a claim, I thought, but man did not forge this boundary marker. It was fashioned by God Himself. It bears His insignia. In man's opinion, this would be a terrible waste. Yet God spared no expense. He gave His best, His most priceless possession.*

> God spared no expense. He gave His most priceless possession.

A sudden flash of light caught my eye. A miniature rainbow beam danced across the page of the architectural drawing, highlighting the surveyor's pin. I turned to see the actual object glistening in the morning sunshine, sunk into the soil where it had been eternally driven. It pulsed with incomparable magnificence, refracting rays of pure brilliance everywhere.

## Gone Fishing

"The entrance!" I gulped, with the consternation of someone already late for an appointment. "He said that we would enter the kingdom today," I exclaimed, the words tumbling out with childlike eagerness. (See Matthew 19:13–15.)

I hastily rerolled the drawings, tightly coiling them so the ribbon would easily slip over the end of the pages, and handed them to one of the angels. Tipping my head forward, I gestured to him. "Keep them nearby. I'll need to refer to them often."

My thoughts raced back to yesterday. Shortly after our arrival on the beach, my entire attention had been focused upon the first surveyor's pin. A gray mist had cloaked the mainland of the kingdom in shadows like a thick curtain upon a mysterious stage. I remembered that darkness had fallen before the cloud had dissipated completely, and I had no hope of seeing beyond the perimeter of this sacred place then.

Now, however, in the light of this glorious morning, everything was visible: the architectural drawings, the surveyor's pin, the footprints in the sand along the beach, the wicker basket. "But wait! Where's the boat?" I asked at the sudden realization that the boat was gone.

A gnawing fear came over me. My eyes looked out over the water with the same intensity as a mother searching the crowd for her wayward toddler, desperate for any sign of Him. Finally, my eyes spied the small craft. I heaved a sigh of relief. There He was, hundreds of yards from shore, standing in the boat as He cast a fishing net into the calm waters. I flung my arms back and forth and shouted, "Jesus, Jesus, You promised to show me the kingdom!"

He waved a reassuring hello and called back, "I'll be there in a moment."

I quickly took stock of my things, checking to be sure my sword was secure at my side and all of the priceless gifts He had given me were still safely enclosed in the shepherd's bag that was fastened to my belt. *I think I'm ready*, I assured myself. *I can't wait to discover what's ahead.*

## No Tourists Allowed

About thirty yards from the beach, massive stone cliffs rose directly in front of us, steep and jagged. Like the walls of an impenetrable fortress, they stretched to the left and right as far as my eyes could see.

"No need for mist," I whispered to myself, looking at the gigantic barrier. "No one could sneak into this place. But there must be a passageway somewhere!"

We stepped past the first golden surveyor's pin toward the interior of the kingdom. An incredible awareness of change overwhelmed me. I felt like a new person. No, I *was* a new person. It was like stepping out of my past into a whole new beginning, an entirely new life.

> It was like stepping out of my past into a new beginning, an entirely new life.

The verse flashed before me: *"If anyone is in Christ, he is a new creation; old things have passed away; behold, all things have become new"* (2 Corinthians 5:17 NKJV).

Jesus turned to the right and made His way along the beach. I followed behind, carefully tracing His footsteps in the sand. We continued to follow the cliff face in silence for several minutes. The metal contents of the leather surveyor's bag slung over Jesus' shoulder clanged together, signaling our progress. Finally, Jesus spoke, "The pathway is just ahead around the turn. Everything has been prepared for our arrival."

*Prepared? What does He mean, "prepared"?* I wondered. My immature concept of simply being a spiritual tourist in His kingdom suddenly vanished.

## Where Are the Keys?

The cliff face turned abruptly to the left. Once we passed the sheer stone abutment, the beach unexpectedly widened into a sizeable, table-flat clearing. In the center of this clearing, a number of large stones of varying size and shape lay piled against each other like building blocks at a construction site.

*These stones didn't just fall here by chance from some precipitous ledge high up on the cliff,* I observed, staring up at the massive stone barrier. *They're piled here intentionally.* The variously shaped stones immediately intrigued me, like pieces of an unsolved jigsaw puzzle waiting to be sorted.

"Come this way, Son," He said, pointing toward the cliff face. "We must lay the foundation stones that lead into My kingdom. These spiritual stones provide the only pathway into My domain. There is no other way."

> "These spiritual stones provide the only pathway into My domain."

Not until we arrived directly in front of the quarried stones could I see what Jesus was pointing to. A narrow fissure, barely large enough for a single person to pass through, split the sheer face of the sea cliff from top to bottom. The tight passageway led straight ahead through the cliff wall into the kingdom. (See Matthew 7:13–14; 27:51.)

The pathway appeared very accessible and inviting. I jumped forward with youthful enthusiasm, intending to rush through the narrow passage. My unrestrained zeal was abruptly checked. Jesus raised His arm in front of me, barring my way. I felt like an impetuous boy being scolded by his father.

"Not so fast, Dale," He cautioned. "This is a spiritual passageway. It requires supernatural keys to enter. Without them, you can go no further." He pointed to the pile of stones.

"But these are stones, Lord," I responded, bewildered. "You said that I need keys in order to pass, not stones."

## Spiritual Stones

"Consult the drawings!" He said firmly.

His words jolted me. *Yes, how foolish of me!* I realized. *But where are the plans? Did the angel obey my instructions?*

A gentle tap on my shoulder answered my question. I turned to find the angel standing behind me, holding the plans for the church in his hands. "Here," he said, stretching them forth. "They are ready for your use."

I spread the drawings open and quickly turned to the second page. The heading read, "The Foundation Stones of the Kingdom." My spirit leapt. A detailed description of six large stones unfolded before my eyes. Beginning at the top of the page, each individual stone was sketched in its proper sequence. I glanced from the drawings to the actual stones piled before me on the sand. The stones perfectly matched the artist's depiction.

*These are no ordinary stones,* I suddenly realized. *They have been fashioned by the hands of the Master Architect. Each one must serve a unique purpose—but how, and where?* I wondered.

The stones had a lifelike quality about them. It reminded me of the *"spiritual rock"* described in the Bible, the one that Moses struck with his rod in the wilderness. (See Exodus 17:6.) Water issued forth from it continuously to quench the thirst of thousands of Israelites. The Bible says that this rock actually followed them for forty years as they journeyed toward the promised land of Canaan. Paul's exact words came to mind: *"And all drank the same spiritual drink. For they drank of that spiritual Rock that followed them, and that Rock was Christ"* (1 Corinthians 10:4 NKJV).

"These are spiritual stones," I affirmed. "They possess supernatural power to transform everyone who touches them. They are alive with God's power and presence. Could these be cut from the Rock of the Lord Himself?" I asked, not daring to approach them.

## Experience Required

Several unusual symbols appeared on the drawing beside each of the stones. My eyes searched the page for a legend explaining their meaning, and then it dawned upon me. "The codebook! It can provide the meaning of these symbols." I quickly loosened the drawstring and reached into my leather pouch to retrieve the green book of symbols that Jesus had given me before we crossed the sea.

I remembered His words of instruction as I eagerly flipped the pages of the booklet. "Each symbol represents an experience in life," Jesus had explained. "When each test is successfully passed, your life experience will unlock the spiritual meaning of that particular symbol. That's the only way you'll be able to interpret My designs and purposes. It's not intellect, it's experience that is required. Only then will I initial your codebook and allow you to proceed further."

Disappointment swept over me like a Christmas missed. The symbols on the drawing were clearly portrayed in my codebook, but no definition followed. There was no signature. Then I realized I was going to have to *experience* these stones before I could understand their true meaning.

## You Must Choose for Yourself

"Are you ready?" Jesus asked. "We have serious work to do. Each of these stones must be carefully laid in their proper order on the pathway into My kingdom. Only then will I permit you to pass into the interior."

He paused. A stern look of serious consequences covered His face, but the slight glimmer in His eyes revealed His hopefulness. "Many have come this far and then turned back," He continued. "Only the few who choose to pay the price will enter this narrow way. You must choose for yourself," He said and then waited in silence for my response.

Like an uncapped fountain bursting forth from deep within me, I cried with joyful enthusiasm. "O Lord, yes!" I answered. "I'm ready. With all my heart I'm ready."

"Then let's begin," He said. "By sunset we should be finished."

# chapter ten

# Supernatural Keys

———◆◦◆◦◆———

W ith a hint of childish enthusiasm, I twisted around in grinning playfulness. "Never have an ordinary day!" I vowed. This motto has served me well. I love the intrigue of investigation. To explore the undiscovered, push beyond the boundaries of the familiar, to never be satisfied with the mundane—ah, yes, that is the spice of living that keeps me young at heart.

*Swiss Family Robinson, Treasure Island, Twenty Thousand Leagues under the Sea, Tom Sawyer, The Chronicles of Narnia, Caravan, South Pacific, The Source, Pale Blue Dot, Amelia Earhart, Charles Lindberg, Yeager*—far more than just adventure stories and biographies, these books, and hundreds more like them, line my library shelves.

They reveal the essence of who I am. Tales of exploration and the challenge to survive, they mirror my enthusiasm for the unknown. In my imagination, I am the one living in the tree house, submerged beneath the sea, eating Turkish Delight, soloing across the world, breaking the sound barrier, and pushing to the edge of the universe.

*The Dayuma Story, Amazing Saints, Through Gates of Splendor, The Cross and the Switchblade, God's Smuggler,*

*The Hiding Place, The Inn of the Sixth Happiness, Jungle Pilot, Chariots of Fire, The Mission, Hudson Taylor, Mother Theresa, Martin Luther King*—chronicles of missionaries on assignment, pressing the edge, going beyond the mundane respectable life of the religious establishment, depicting lives that are *extraordinary.* These are a just a few of the religious pilgrims, the spiritual trailblazers, whose footsteps I pursue on the path of spiritual adventure and discovery.

In my journeys, both natural and spiritual, I have often recalled these words that Charles Kuralt wrote:

> But, if the traveler expects the highway to be safe and well graded, he might as well stay home. The little roads without numbers are the ones I have liked best, the bumpy ones that lead over the hills toward vicinities unknown.[1]

## Unexpected Conviction

*"Never have an ordinary day"* is about to take on a whole *new meaning,* I considered, bracing myself for the work ahead. *Today certainly fits the bill. The territory we're entering surpasses anything that I can describe in familiar terms. What we're about to undertake goes far beyond my natural senses.* My fingers twitched with anticipation. *We're in the realm of the supernatural here. I have no idea what to expect!*

Never have an ordinary day!

Jesus and I stood on opposite sides of the first stone. It was large and flat. He nodded His approval as we bent together to lift it from its place on top of the pile. *This is the first supernatural stone,* I thought, bracing myself for the unexpected.

The instant I touched the granular surface of the stone, a sudden surge of self-examination swept through me. Feelings and emotions began to surface within my spirit, evoking a powerful sense of conviction for things I had done in the past. Snapshots of neglected opportunities, moments of rebellious disobedience, and times of downright sinful behavior flashed before me.

> A powerful sense of conviction for things I had done in the past flooded over me.

*What's happening to me?* I thought, confused. *Simply touching this stone is having a spiritual impact. I feel such conviction!*

Jesus looked over at me with a discerning expression of understanding as we struggled to maneuver the heavy stone toward the narrow passageway. It took all my strength to steady the flat rectangular rock. I stumbled several times in the soft sand of the beach under its burden.

Jesus was not deterred by my human weakness. "We're almost there," He encouraged. "A few more paces and we'll have it in place."

My grip tightened around the edge of the supernatural object. The pronounced roughness of the surface was so abrasive that it tore at my fleshy fingertips—to such an extent that I realized its deeply grooved surface would cause the feet of those who might step upon it to twist and turn.

## The First Golden Key

We set the stone in place at the entrance of the narrow pathway. *It's impossible for anyone to proceed past the cliff face into the kingdom without stepping upon this stone,* I thought.

Immediately, Jesus reached into the leather surveyor's bag and withdrew a chisel that looked something like a branding iron. The metal stamp had an insignia on the end of it.

He handed me the tool along with the golden hammer and said, "Mark the stone with this insignia. This is the stone of repentance. All who seek to enter My kingdom must first step here!"

I placed the masonry tool on the abrasive surface of the stone and struck it with all my might. The sudden sound of the impact reverberated through the narrow passageway and faded into the interior of the kingdom. When I lifted the chisel, an imprint was clearly visible, permanently set into the grainy stone surface. I stared, transfixed, watching in amazement as the perfectly engraved image mysteriously changed color. A golden metallic glow began to radiate from the symbol. It was a golden key.

"It is established for all eternity," Jesus said. "It is immoveable. No one can ever adjust or change it. Stepping upon this stone will reveal all sin and ungodliness. It will bring immediate conviction of guilt and godly sorrow. It will evoke emotional pain, heartache, and deep feelings of uncleanness. Those who stand upon this stone will clearly see their spiritual condition. They cannot hide from the reality of who they are and what they have done; it is undeniable. My Holy Spirit draws all mankind to this place of conviction."

> **Stepping on this stone will reveal all sin and ungodliness.**

Jesus' words from the Scripture flashed into my mind:

*And I, if I am lifted up from the earth, will draw all men to Myself.* (John 12:32)

*But I tell you the truth, it is to your advantage that I go away; for if I do not go away, the Helper will not come to you; but if I go, I will send Him to you. And He, when He comes, will convict the world concerning sin and righteousness and judgment; concerning sin, because they do not believe in Me; and concerning righteousness, because I go to the Father and you no longer see Me; and concerning judgment, because the ruler of this world has been judged.* (John 16:7–11)

*No one can come to Me unless the Father who sent Me draws him.* (John 6:44)

## A Place of Repentance

*Dare I test this first stone?* I wondered as I stood up to examine the finished work. I raised my foot to step onto it. I hesitated only an instant; Jesus' approval was obvious.

The moment my foot touched the surface, it twisted, pulled by an unseen power, toward the kingdom. Suddenly, I saw myself as a teenager back in my home church. The scene, forever imprinted upon my memory, was so real. I could hear the evangelist, his crutches leaning against the dark oak pulpit, powerfully proclaiming the Gospel. His crippled legs, a result of polio, did not hinder the anointing of God as he spoke plainly about the fact that all have sinned and come short of the glory of God. He called for a repentant heart, a change of life, a decision to turn from sin and the world to follow Jesus Christ.

> It was a call for a repentant heart, a change of life, a decision to turn from the world and follow Christ.

It felt as if I were the only person in the church. His words stung my conscience and penetrated into my heart. Inescapable conviction swept over me. I realized that I was a sinner and I desperately needed forgiveness. My life was headed down the wrong path. Without a doubt, I knew that if I kept going in this direction, my life would end in pain and tragedy.

*Jesus died for my sins.* The reality of this truth burst into my life for the first time. *I need Jesus in my life right now! I dare not wait another second.* When the invitation was given to accept Christ, I leapt from my seat and ran forward.

Tears poured from my eyes as I knelt at the altar. For more than twenty minutes, I wept uncontrollably as Jesus washed away my sins, transforming my life. When I finally stood up, I was a different person. The old things had passed away. Everything was new. I was headed in the right direction!

My friends and youth leaders were eager to welcome me into God's family. One of the adult leaders approached me with a jubilant smile on her face. "How do you feel now?" she asked.

> I felt clean for the first time in my life!

"I feel clean for the first time in my life!" I replied, experiencing the sense of innocence that only God can give.

My life was totally transformed in that moment. Genuine repentance had transpired. I was more than just sorry for my sins. I wanted a new life. I was willing—no, I was desperate—to change. I had taken my first step toward God's kingdom, the step of repentance. I would never be the same.

## Turning toward Home

I stepped from the supernatural surface, quivering with the discovery of new spiritual truth. I stared at the amazing stone set in the path. "Now I understand," I said. "Repentance is the first step of this incredible journey into His kingdom. It is the turning point, a 180 degree change in direction from my own kingdom toward the lordship of Jesus Christ."

Jesus' words resounded in my spirit: *"The time is fulfilled, and the kingdom of God is at hand; repent and believe in the gospel"* (Mark 1:15).

"Lord, thank You for Your mercy and grace that drew me to this place of repentance years ago," I said, looking at Jesus.

## Nothing Seems Impossible

Jesus hastened back to the pile of stones with surprising urgency. *It must be important to set the next stone in place as quickly as possible,* I surmised. The moment I touched it, my heart leapt. It was much lighter than the first one, requiring little effort to lift. Doubt and unbelief drained out of me. *This is so wonderful,* I thought, glancing over at the Lord.

Faith became suddenly tangible, identifiable, and even substantive; I was touching and handling it. I felt so full of faith in God that nothing seemed impossible or undoable. *I never want to let go of this stone,* I decided, gripping it with greater determination.

We set the rock down onto the smooth pathway with its edge touching the stone of repentance. Jesus knelt down, and for a long time He carefully examined the two stones to insure that there was no separation between them.

## His Word, a Stone

*What's He doing?* I questioned. *I must refer to the drawings.* I turned momentarily toward the angel who immediately held them open for me to see. The architectural plans gave clear details regarding this second spiritual stone. The caption read, "A Sure Foundation Stone."

Turning back toward the pathway, I watched in amazement as the stone settled into the soil. It appeared to be resting on bedrock. "It's immovable!" I confessed. "This stone is absolutely trustworthy. No matter what weight I place on it, it will not budge. Surely, this stone is set on an unshakable foundation." (See Isaiah 28:16; Hebrews 11:3.)

> This stone, the Word of God, is absolutely trustworthy.

I watched in astonishment as writing mysteriously appeared on the face of the stone. The message read, "The Word of God, Unchanging, Immoveable, Eternal. The Word Become Flesh, the Son of God."

"So that's it!" I blurted out, confident that I understood the inscription. "This stone rests upon the eternal Word of

163

God, and He cannot lie. His Word is irrefutable. He keeps every promise. What God says, He will do." (See 2 Corinthians 1:20.)

Paul's words raced through my thoughts. He spoke so clearly about the relationship between the Word and faith:

> *But what does it say? "THE WORD IS NEAR YOU, in your mouth and in your heart"—that is, the word of faith which we are preaching, that if you confess with your mouth Jesus as Lord, and believe in your heart that God raised Him from the dead, you will be saved; for with the heart a person believes, resulting in righteousness, and with the mouth he confesses, resulting in salvation. For the Scripture says, "WHOEVER BELIEVES IN HIM WILL NOT BE DISSAPPOINTED." For there is no distinction between Jew and Greek; for the same Lord is Lord of all, abounding in riches for all who call on Him; for "WHOEVER WILL CALL ON THE NAME OF THE LORD WILL BE SAVED." How then will they call on Him in whom they have not believed? How will they believe in Him whom they have not heard? And how will they hear without a preacher? How will they preach unless they are sent? Just as it is written, "HOW BEAUTIFUL ARE THE FEET OF THOSE WHO BRING GOOD NEWS OF GOOD THINGS!" However, they did not all heed the good news; for Isaiah says, "LORD, WHO HAS BELIEVED OUR REPORT?" So faith comes from hearing, and hearing by the word of Christ.*
> (Romans 10:8–17)

## Faith-Walkers

Jesus glanced toward the hammer and chisel and then at me. *I must engrave the stone,* I thought and immediately reached for the implements. I struck the chisel with a sense of confidence. The same image was hammered into the stone's face, but this time an unexpected sound was released.

Music instantly filled the atmosphere. It originated within the kingdom. The lyrics penetrated into the far end of the narrow passageway. "He is faithful; He is the Faithful One," came the assuring refrain over and over. I listened to the enthralling song, my spirit absorbing each verse. Again and again the phrase resounded, each time with increasing volume. Then, culminating in one final crescendo of affirmation, the concluding chorus came like a finale of truth: "In Him there is only Yes and Amen!" (See 2 Corinthians 1:20.)

"We must walk by faith, not by sight," I confessed as I fixed my attention on Jesus. (See 2 Corinthians 5:7.)

> We must walk by faith, not by sight.

"Yes," He responded. "All who enter My kingdom must be faith-walkers. This is what My apostles teach and what My Word declares. This is the second step on the pathway that leads into My kingdom. All who enter here must do so by faith." (See Ephesians 2:1–10.)

## Someone Please Help Me!

I stood on the beach next to Jesus, hopelessly staring at the third stone in the dwindling pile. *I'll never be able to move this,* I thought, in a serious quandary. *It's over six feet long. There's no way I can lift it without supernatural assistance.*

The huge rock resembled a rectangular boulder rather than the flat, manageable fieldstone normally used for a pathway. Its top surface was gouged away giving it the appearance of a drinking trough. I looked at Jesus with a sense of helplessness. "What can I do, Lord?" I shrugged.

"This stone requires the help of others," He replied. "All who enter My kingdom must have the assistance of My servants when they approach this stone." (See Matthew 28:19; Acts 8:26–40.)

He motioned to our angelic companions, and they quickly stepped toward the boulder. Together we lifted the huge stone. It wasn't a pretty sight; I wheezed and spluttered, with knees buckling, toward the narrow passageway. I was more than happy to release the burden. It sank into the soft soil, coming to rest flush with the surface of the pathway.

*This is amazing,* I thought. *God's ways are certainly not my ways. If I were constructing a pathway, I sure wouldn't do it like this. But this is a supernatural pathway,* I reminded myself. *This is God's perfect design.*

*It's impossible to proceed through this passageway without stepping down into this stone. You have to descend into this trough and step out on the other side,* I puzzled, trying to figure out its supernatural purpose.

## He Is the Water

Still breathless from the weight of the stone, I set the chisel upon the surface of the rock and struck it with the gold hammer. Miraculously, the hollow basin filled with water from some unknown source, as if I had turned a faucet on and the fountains of the deep were broken open by the force of my blow.

When I lifted the tool from the surface, I noticed that the key emblazoned upon the rock was a different color than the first one. This insignia was pure white.

To my surprise, Jesus immediately stepped into the pool of water. Suddenly, I realized what I was witnessing. All who enter His kingdom must pass through this water, and He was the first to do so! (See Matthew 3:1–17; Romans 6:1–14.)

## Filled with Praise and Power

A gentle wind began to blow from within the kingdom. Its force gradually increased as it surged through the narrow passageway and swirled above the basin. I was engulfed in this rushing, roaring wind. Its force enveloped me with such vigor that I felt empowered in my spirit. It was energizing, like a powerful charge of electric current pulsating through me. And then suddenly it ceased.

I felt an ecstatic, overwhelming sense of God's power and presence. A desire to worship filled my being. "You are awesome, God!" I shouted shamelessly. "There is no one like You doing wonders and miracles. You are altogether righteous. Your mercy is everlasting. Your love is new every morning. You are beautiful in Your holiness." The praise was unstoppable. It flowed from me like a river overflowing its banks, flooding the land with pure worship. There was a worship service going on inside of me! I was alive with His power and presence. The eternal witness of His resurrection coursed through my being. (See Acts 1–2.)

> A worship service was going on inside me!

## The Place of Surrender

"All who enter My kingdom must pass through the water and through the wind that swirls above this stone," Jesus said as He stepped from the basin. "This is the stone of baptisms. (See 1 Corinthians 10:1–2.) This stone is set in the exact place of demarcation that seals My lordship.

"Many choose to view My kingdom from afar," He explained. "They are the ones who have passed the first surveyor's pin. They have repented and believe that I am the Son of God. They have entered the pathway but have stopped short of the kingdom." He was adamant. "Only those who pass through this stone truly *enter* the kingdom of God." (See John 3:5.)

He continued, "This is the stone of My lordship! It is the place of death and burial to worldly allegiances and to the kingdom of self. It is the place of resurrection into supernatural life under My sovereign authority.

"Those who refuse to pass beyond this stone can only see My kingdom from a distance," He said with frustration. The severity of His words left no alternative.

"I am much more than Savior; I am Lord! Only those who have acknowledged Me as their Lord will enter fully into My domain.

"This is the place of delineation," He declared, leaving no room for ambiguity. "This is the point of transition from seeing to entering! This is the stone of My lordship, which produces the circumcision of the heart. It does away with the old nature and produces the new. It is the place of cleansing and government." (See Colossians 2:11–14.)

## Born of Water and Spirit

Jesus' instructions to Nicodemus flashed through my mind: *"Unless one is born again he cannot see the kingdom of God....Unless one is born of water and the Spirit he cannot enter into the kingdom of God"* (John 3:3, 5). It made perfect sense now. Baptism is the place of *entrance* into His Lordship!

I turned to examine the architectural drawings of the church. A previously unnoticed, all-important detail leapt from the page. A bold line was drawn across the pathway directly through the stone of baptisms. On one side of the line it was only possible to *see* into the kingdom. To proceed beyond the line was to *embrace* God's sovereignty.

> This is where we die!

"This is where we die!" I said.

## The First Doorkeeper

*God's design is perfect,* I thought, as I studied the remarkable drawings. *He's the Master Architect. He made us in His image. He loves us so much. He devised a wonderful plan to redeem us and restore us to Himself. Not only has He opened the way into the place of intimacy with Him, He has created a path into His kingdom.*

"Do you understand the significance of the keys that you have imprinted on each of these stones?" Jesus said, startling me back into the awareness of His presence.

"I think so," I replied tentatively, not wanting to assume anything.

"Do you remember My conversation with Simon?"

"Which one, Lord?"

"When I asked him the question, 'Who do you say that I am?'"

"Yes, I remember."

"His response was beyond human knowledge. My Father gave Him the answer."

"'You are the Christ, the Son of the living God!" I interrupted.

> You are the Christ, the Son of the living God!

"I have established my church upon this truth," He continued. "No other foundation is necessary. Right then and there I changed Simon's name to Peter. I chose him as the first one to receive the keys to My kingdom. (See Matthew 16:15–19.)

"The images that you have engraved on the stones along this pathway represent the keys that I gave to Peter. He used them for the first time on the Day of Pentecost. When the multitudes were convicted of their sins by his anointed preaching and the presence of My Holy Spirit, they cried out, *'What shall we do?'* (Acts 2:37).

"Peter knew it was the appointed time. He used the spiritual keys to open the way into My kingdom. He told the crowd, *'Repent, and each of you be baptized in the name of Jesus Christ for the forgiveness of your sins; and you will receive the gift of the Holy Spirit'* (Acts 2:38).

"Peter was the first doorkeeper," Jesus said with finality, "but these three keys still unlock the way."

## The Good News

"My message has always been the good news of My kingdom!" He continued. "It is My mission. I *will* build My church, and the gates of hell will not prevail against it. All things will be subdued under My lordship." (See Matthew 16:18 KJV.)

The profound truth of Jesus' words penetrated my spirit. I looked at the three stones that were carefully designed for the pathway into His kingdom. "Lord," I said, "this is the path that I have chosen. Repentance, faith, and baptism in water and the Holy Spirit are my own personal experience. Your invisible kingdom is so real to me. You have opened my spiritual eyes."

> I knelt in the narrow passageway in submission to the King.

I knelt in the narrow passageway in submission to the King. "What Paul wrote is true," I acknowledged. "You are Lord of the dead and the living. I bow my knee and humbly confess that You are Lord." I paused, and then with well thought-out determination, I declared my allegiance: "Jesus, You are *my* Lord and *my* King." (See Romans 14:9; Philippians 2:10–11; and Psalm 84:3.)

## Deliver the Message

"This is the message you must declare everywhere that I send you," He replied. "These are your marching orders: 'Go into all the world and preach the good news of the kingdom to every creature. He who believes and is baptized will be saved; but he who does not believe will be condemned.'" (See Mark 16:15–16 NKJV.) "Freely give them the keys to My kingdom. Point them to the narrow path that leads into My power and purpose."

## The Keys Are for You

The world of dreams and visions faded. [2] Jesus words grew distant. Discharged from the place of intimacy with Him, I carefully recorded His instructions in my journal. I knew I must deliver this urgent message to whomever might read these words in the years to come.

The very same keys that Peter used to open the way into God's kingdom on the day of Pentecost will work in your life right now. The Gospel is the good news of God's government. It is the wonderful message that Jesus Christ is Savior *and* Lord. Only He has the power to forgive your sins. Not only does He have the power, but because He is Lord, He also has the authority to do exactly that.

Jesus not only came into this world to save you from sin, but He also came to establish His kingdom in your life! This is His purpose. The King has an incredible plan for your life. Your destiny can only be fulfilled as you embrace His right to reign and submit to His lordship.

> Jesus came to establish His kingdom in your life.

Your first step of obedience is baptism. Through baptism we are buried with Him and raised with Him into His kingdom, where His authority is absolute. We are no longer our own. We are bought with a price, His blood. As the apostle Paul put it, we are bondslaves of Jesus Christ. We joyfully *choose* to submit to His lordship.

## The Kingdom Is Waiting

Paul wrote, *"The kingdom of God is not eating and drinking, but righteousness and peace and joy in the Holy Spirit"* (Romans 14:17). Make no mistake: the kingdom of God is *"in the Holy Spirit."* We are born *of* the Spirit, and it is the baptism *in* the Holy Spirit that releases God's supernatural power in our lives. This is why Jesus said to

His followers, "Wait until you receive power from on high." (See Luke 24:49.) It is impossible to fulfill your destiny and assignment in God's kingdom without the enabling power of the Holy Spirit.

Paul described the kingdom in this order: First comes *righteousness*—genuine repentance and authentic faith in Christ result in righteousness, or *right relationships* between God and man. The consequence of this rightness is *peace*. His peace brings *joy*. Once this divine order of righteousness, peace, and joy is established in our lives, it's time to get busy doing the work of the kingdom. Jesus said, "These things shall you do, and greater things than these shall you do, because I go to My Father." (See John 14:12.)

The kingdom of God awaits you! The power of God is available to you right now. Don't stop short of the fullness of God's purpose. Don't settle outside on the fringes of God's awesome kingdom. Don't just view it from a distance. Come on in!

> Don't stop short of the fullness of God's purpose or settle outside on the fringes of His kingdom.

He invites you to step through the waters of baptism into His supernatural kingdom. Call your pastor and ask Him to baptize you in water today. Ask Jesus to baptize you in the Holy Spirit.

Become an empowered witness and soldier in God's army. Surrender your allegiance to Jesus Christ. Not only is He your Savior; He is also your King!

I couldn't wait to return to the well of His presence to finish the pathway.

## chapter eleven

# Elementary Principles

◆ ◆ ◆ ◆

W e've completed half of the pathway," Jesus said, as we retraced our steps back to the pile of unused stones remaining on the beach. Large beads of sweat formed on my brow in the noonday heat. They dripped onto the top stone with an audible splat, leaving small dark circles on its gray surface. The smell of freshly turned soil emanated from the moist droplet stains, like pungent air from a newly plowed field. Lifting this fourth stone from the stack, we carried it toward the narrow passageway into the kingdom.

## Marching Orders

"I can't keep my grip," I complained in frustration, struggling to keep hold of the rock's edge.

*This stone is acting strangely. Its shape keeps changing,* I thought, repositioning my hands for the third time. *It's pliable like clay, responsive to the slightest pressure.* My fingers kept leaving impressions where my hands grasped the malleable surface.

We maneuvered the stone into position at the far end of the pathway. Jesus stood to examine the details of the completed work.

"This is one of the first principles," He said, piquing my curiosity.

"First principles?" I asked, with obvious fascination.

"Yes," He replied. "When you enter My kingdom you receive a specific assignment. Every one of My servants must obtain their marching orders. This is essential; the information will clarify your call and duties as My disciple."

"Marching orders?" I questioned, placing my weight momentarily on the stone. When I stepped away, both of my feet had left clear impressions in the clay. I watched in amazement as the imprint gradually disappeared and the surface returned to its original shape. "What is this?" I blurted out, perplexed by the abnormal reaction of the stone. I immediately turned toward the angel to examine the architectural blueprints for an answer.

## Prophetic Insight

The drawing accurately depicted the fourth stone. A notation alongside the artistic sketch described its characteristics. The caption read, "Prophetic Release." Beneath it a list of qualities followed: Destiny, Calling, Gifting, Revelation, and Impartation.

We receive confirmation about our assignments and supernatural impartation to accomplish them.

*How exciting!* I thought. *This stone is the place of release into ministry. Like a spiritual launching pad, here is where we receive confirmation about our assignments and supernatural impartation to accomplish our mission.*

I turned and knelt beside the stone, holding the chisel lightly against the sensitive surface. The hammer blow drove it deep into the stone's interior. To my surprise, the indentation immediately solidified, becoming granite hard. The symbol of the key was permanently set deep into the rock.

The embossed image imprinted in the clay captivated me. The dazzling key began to release a fascinating rainbow of colors, which emanated from deep within the stone.

I saw a kaleidoscope of intricate designs, the patterns never duplicated themselves; they kept evolving and changing. The continuous array testified to God's unlimited creativity.

"This is the stone of the laying on of hands," Jesus said. "It is a prophetic stone. This is where I give direction to My servants regarding their specific assignments. All my soldiers must receive clear orders so that they can function successfully in My army. Everyone who enters My kingdom must pass this stone. It is vital to their success. That's why I have placed it here at the entrance." [1]

## Impartation

Quite unexpectedly, Jesus stretched out His hands and placed them upon my head. Revelation exploded within me. I felt like clay being molded and shaped by the Master Potter. As He prayed, His purpose poured into me. My spirit leapt with affirmation. A powerful, supernatural release into a whole new unexpected sphere of calling and ministry exploded inside of me.

"Son," He said, "I impart to you the anointing that you need for the work ahead. Receive My grace and commission. Embrace My heart of compassion and love for My church. I release to you an understanding of My designs and the structure of My government. From this day forward, I commission you to go and build My church. Proclaim My kingdom! Fulfill your ministry by My authority. Walk in your assignment with joy and courage."

## Spiritual Clarity

Clarity flooded into my life. Any uncertainty about my calling was gone, totally banished by the authority of Jesus' words. I stood to my feet, powerfully motivated by prophetic revelation. I felt edified and released. Jesus' exhortation brought not only great encouragement, but comfort as well. (See 1 Corinthians 14:3.)

"My assignment in His kingdom is crystal-clear," I affirmed. "No matter what opposition I may encounter, it will not succeed. I am empowered by Your prophetic words of calling and commission."

Paul's words of encouragement to Timothy, his spiritual son in the Lord, scrolled through my mind, further solidifying my resolve:

> Let no one despise your youth, but be an example to the believers in word, in conduct, in love, in spirit, in faith, in purity. Till I come, give attention to reading, to exhortation, to doctrine. Do not neglect the gift that is in you, which was given to you by prophecy with the laying on of the hands of the eldership....Therefore I remind you to stir up the gift of God which is in you through the laying on of my hands. For God has not given us a spirit of fear, but of power and of love and of a sound mind....But you be watchful in all things, endure afflictions, do the work of an evangelist, fulfill your ministry.
>
> (1 Timothy 4:12–14; 2 Timothy 1:6–7; 4:5 NKJV)

Through the Word, I knew that one purpose for the laying on of hands is to confer a blessing or an inheritance upon others. (See Genesis 48:12–16.) A second reason is for healing. Jesus gave clear instructions that we are to lay hands on the sick and they shall recover. (See Mark 16:18.)

> The laying on of hands confers blessing and imparts direction.

*But this is different*, I pondered. *This "laying on of hands" is for impartation and direction for every believer who enters the kingdom of God. Jesus was insistent about placing this fourth stone at the entrance into His kingdom. It's essential to our success as His servants.*

## The Transfer of Power and Authority

"I'm convinced!" I nodded with affirmation. "This is where God's soldiers are commissioned and released into service. It's foundational, and it's for *all* His children!"

Scenes from church history flashed before me: the blessings and inheritance of Abraham, Isaac, and Jacob granted to their sons by the laying on of hands; the transfer of power and authority from Moses to Joshua; the anointing of Saul and David as kings of Israel by the prophet Samuel; the commissioning of the disciples to go and preach the good news of the kingdom; spiritual fathers and mothers, church leaders and presbyteries, pastors and prophets—all imparting a blessing by the laying on of their hands, prophetically conferring a Holy Spirit-initiated direction and anointing.

A holy boldness overwhelmed me. "Listen up!" I shouted into the air toward the empty beach, like a drill sergeant in the Marine Corps addressing new recruits. "This is the stone of the laying on of hands. You *will* report here for your orders. No soldier of Christ will proceed to duty without first receiving his or her assignment. Do you hear me, soldier?"

## By His Hands

I felt foolish after the sudden outburst, but gratitude quickly displaced my embarrassment. "Jesus, You truly are the Master Potter, and we are the clay," I said, looking up into His eyes of wisdom. "You summon all Your children here to this place of commissioning. You use chosen and anointed leaders as Your hands to shape us and release us into our calling and destiny."

"Yes," He replied. "That's why this stone must be part of the beginning. It's foundational to life in My kingdom."

> God wants to commission you as His servant.

A voice out of spiritual history echoed into my spirit. *"Whom shall I send, and who will go for Us?"* came the celestial question. Isaiah responded to God's invitation. He reported for duty: *"Here am I. Send me!"* (Isaiah 6:8).

Do you hear God asking you the same question right now? Will you report for duty? What is your response to the

177

voice of His Spirit? He wants to commission you as His servant.

## Touching Life

The remaining stones lay across each other like colossal pick-up sticks. *Two more to go, and we'll be finished,* I thought. *I can't wait to complete this pathway so we can go on into the kingdom. First things first, though,* I sighed with a hint of impatience.

I positioned myself at one end of the unusual seven-foot-long, column-shaped stone and discovered to my amazement that it was hollow. Jesus stood at the opposite end.

"Are you ready?" He asked.

"It looks impossible to me, but I'm willing to try." I responded.

"With Me, all things are possible," He said as He touched the stone. (See Matthew 19:26.)

*I think He's implying something more here,* I thought, not realizing that He was preparing me for what was about to happen.

## The Shock of My Life

The moment I grasped the fifth stone, the life force of God impacted my flesh. It felt like I was gripping a high-voltage electric wire with my bare hands while standing in a pool of water. The stone became a spiritual conduit. The surge of power knocked the wind out of me. My chest sank in, my arms stiffened, and my hands clenched tightly to the hollow cylindrical column. Enlivening energy pulsed into me with energizing vigor.

Life passed before my grimacing eyes: a sudden flashback, a snapshot of an open tomb, the face of Lazarus, a millisecond of some unleashed power quickening the dead. I gasped for air, struggling for life.

All the things that Jesus taught me about life raced through my mind like pages from a scrapbook: the moment in creation when God breathed life into Adam and Eve; the Tree of Life in the center of the Garden of Eden; a multitude of children, babies birthed generation after generation, millions upon millions of lives. It was an overwhelming, inundating view of mankind being endued with the life of God, the impartation of life force from the beginning of creation until the present moment. [2]

I struggled to find a word adequate to describe this electrifying sensation: creation, consciousness, awareness, existence, responsiveness, touch, sound, taste, smell, sight, perception, thought, reason, emotion, feeling, love, joy, pain, sadness, longing, wonder, curiosity, being...*life*.

"Life—that's it!" I shouted, still pulsating with the vibrant, infusion of energy.

Life—
that's it!

Jesus' words scrolled through my mind:

*I am the way, and the truth, and the **life**....I came that they may have **life**, and have it abundantly....I am the resurrection and the **life**; he who believes in Me will **live** even if he dies, and everyone who **lives** and believes in Me will never die....As the Father has **life** in Himself, even so He gave to the Son also to have **life** in Himself...come to Me so that you may have **life**....for the bread of God is He who comes down from heaven and gives **life** to the world....I am the bread of life.* [3]

The potent realization of life in Jesus downloaded into my spirit. *I'm somehow touching life through this supernatural stone,* I realized, looking across the conduit into the gleaming face of Jesus. "In Him is life, and the life is the Light of men," I whispered, awestruck by His power. (See John 1:4.)

## A Spiritual Vortex

We maneuvered the stone into position at the far end of the pathway. The moment we let go of it, the long cylinder began to spin, rotating with increasing speed until its high velocity made it appear motionless.

*How will I ever mark this stone with the engraving tool?* I wondered. *It's moving so fast I dare not touch it.*

Before I could complete my thought, Jesus lifted the hammer and chisel and approached the stone Himself. He boldly struck it near the hollow opening. Instantly, the column grew larger, expanding in circumference until it became a tunnel; a spiritual vortex was created, a sort of black hole leading beyond this world of imprisoned time, where everything returns to ashes and dust and death is inevitable.

A large piece from the side of the column broke away and spun crashing against the wall of the cliff in the narrow passageway. There it lay, resting against the shear wall of the chasm, looking in every way like one of the stones used to seal an ancient tomb in the East. To my utter amazement, the embossed key was clearly engraved upon the face of the tomb door.

## Standing on the Resurrection

"This is the stone of resurrection!" He said. His very words filled me with hope. "It imparts life to all who enter into My kingdom. Those who tread upon this stone walk in absolute confidence of resurrection life, in this world as well as in the world to come!

The stone of resurrection imparts life to all who enter.

"All doubt must be banished," He continued. "Belief in My resurrection is a prerequisite in My kingdom. Without faith in the Resurrection, you will end up disillusioned and hopelessly lost in misery."

*It's obvious why He had to mark the stone and set the seal Himself,* I suddenly realized. *He's the only one qualified to open the way through the path of death into life. He possesses the keys of death and hell. The door is open; we follow in His footsteps.*

## There Can Be No Doubt

"But why must this stone be placed here at the entrance?" I asked.

"Don't you see?" He replied. "My resurrection is the undeniable verification of who I am. It was necessary for the first apostles to see Me alive after My death so they could testify with absolute certainty that I am alive.

"This is why I appeared to the apostle Paul in person, so that he could tell the Gentiles that I am risen from the dead. He bore witness as one who saw firsthand. My apostles are *eyewitnesses* to the indisputable fact that I am alive. They have seen and believe!

"The power of the Resurrection is the power of the kingdom," He concluded with the finality of an attorney closing His case.

It was as if the Lord opened a tap, and all doubt concerning life after death drained out of me. "Jesus, You opened the door. It can never be closed," I affirmed. "The dead will rise again!"

## The Power of the Kingdom

Paul's words of rebuke to the Corinthians took on fresh potency:

*Now if Christ is preached, that He has been raised from the dead, how do some among you say that there is no resurrection of the dead? But if there is no resurrection of the dead, not even Christ has been raised; and if Christ has not been raised, then our preaching is vain, your faith also is vain. Moreover we are even found to be*

181

*false witnesses of God, because we testified against God that He raised Christ, whom He did not raise, if in fact the dead are not raised. For if the dead are not raised, not even Christ has been raised; and if Christ has not been raised, your faith is worthless; you are still in your sins. Then those also who have fallen asleep in Christ have perished. If we have hoped in Christ in this life only, we are of all men most to be pitied. But now Christ has been raised from the dead, the first fruits of those who are asleep. For since by a man came death, by a man also came the resurrection of the dead. For as in Adam all die, so also in Christ all will be made alive.*
(1 Corinthians 15:12–22)

## This Is Not an Option

"That's why I felt such power when I touched the stone, Lord," I said. "Your life-giving power was surging through my body. That certainly puts fresh light on Paul's words."

*However, you are not in the flesh but in the Spirit, if indeed the Spirit of God dwells in you. But if anyone does not have the Spirit of Christ, he does not belong to Him. If Christ is in you, though the body is dead because of sin, yet the spirit is alive because of righteousness. But if the Spirit of Him who raised Jesus from the dead dwells in you, He who raised Christ Jesus from the dead will also give life to your mortal bodies through His Spirit who dwells in you.* (Romans 8:9–11)

The profound significance of this stone settled into my spirit. Belief in the Resurrection is not an option. It is fundamental to life in the kingdom of God. If there is no resurrection, then our faith is in vain and our labor is futile.

Because He lives, we shall live also. We are called to serve a risen Savior. In God's kingdom there is no death, only life! We must understand this from the beginning, at the entrance into His kingdom. He is the God of the living, not the dead. We walk in resurrection life!

# chapter twelve
# Border Guards

---◆◦◆◦◆---

*O*ne more stone to go, I thought, turning toward the beach and the setting sun where the orphaned stone still lay. *Once it's in place, we can proceed into the interior of God's hidden domain.* In eager anticipation, I said aloud, "I can't wait to discover the secrets of God's kingdom."

I grasped the stone with presumptuous eagerness. My hands jerked back instantly as I recoiled in shock. It felt as if I had just grabbed a razor-sharp piece of coral. I anxiously examined my fingers, looking for an open wound. Relieved to see that they were not sliced open, I studied the stone's surface. It was extremely hard and as sharp as a surgeon's knife.

Reluctant to touch the stone again, I looked at Jesus with a troubled expression. "How will I lift this, Lord?" I asked. "I can't touch it without getting cut."

## Do Not Touch

"Stand aside, Son," He said, with a look of displeasure. "You shouldn't have touched it in the first place. I'll carry this one Myself. Follow Me to the end of the pathway; you can help Me once the stone is set in place."

With a fearless boldness that defied logic, He picked the stone up and supported its heavy weight on His shoulder. (See Isaiah 9:6.) A look of clear discernment glistened in His eyes as He strode through the narrow passageway to the end of the path and dropped the stone into position on the ground next to the resurrection stone. Stepping beyond it onto the soil of the kingdom, He pointed to the hammer and chisel.

"Engrave the stone!" He said. "It is set here for all eternity."

I raised the hammer and struck the chisel with all my might in an attempt to compensate for the unyielding hardness of the stone. To my utter horror, the chisel broke in my hand, sending sparks flying. The engraving tool was beyond repair.

"O Lord, I'm sorry," I cried.

"The chisel will no longer be needed," He responded.

I let out a huge sigh. I was relieved to see that the imbedded impression of the key was clearly visible on the steel-hard surface.

"This is the last stone, the final key marking the entrance to the kingdom of God," Jesus said.

## Inescapable Judgment

"This is the stone of eternal judgment." He spoke with a tone of finality. "It completes the pathway into My kingdom."

> The stone of eternal judgment completes the pathway into the kingdom.

"Eternal judgment!" I uttered. "No wonder it felt like my flesh was torn open when I touched it."

The Holy Spirit immediately drew my attention to Paul's words to the Romans and to the Corinthians:

*Therefore you have no excuse, everyone of you who passes judgment, for in that which you judge another, you condemn yourself; for you who judge practice the same things. And we know that the judgment of God rightly falls upon those who practice such things. But do you suppose this, O man, when you pass judgment on those who practice such things and do the same yourself, that you will escape the judgment of God? Or do you think lightly of the riches of His kindness and tolerance and patience, not knowing that the kindness of God leads you to repentance? But because of your stubbornness and unrepentant heart you are storing up wrath for yourself in the day of wrath and revelation of the righteous judgment of God, who* WILL RENDER TO EACH PERSON ACCORDING TO HIS DEEDS: *to those who by perseverance in doing good seek for glory and honor and immortality, eternal life; but to those who are selfishly ambitious and do not obey the truth, but obey unrighteousness, wrath and indignation. There will be tribulation and distress for every soul of man who does evil, of the Jew first and also of the Greek, but glory and honor and peace to everyone who does good, to the Jew first and also to the Greek. For there is no partiality with God....on the day when, according to my gospel, God will judge the secrets of men through Christ Jesus.*
(Romans 2:1–11, 16)

*Therefore we also have as our ambition...to be pleasing to Him. For we must all appear before the judgment seat of Christ, so that each one may be recompensed for his deeds in the body, according to what he has done, whether good or bad.* (2 Corinthians 5:9–10)

Reflecting on the truth of what he had written, I thought, *Paul was aware of the imminent judgment that all mankind would ultimately face; it was critical to his life and thinking and, no doubt, motivated him to live a holy life.*

## Accountability in the Kingdom

One final burst of information unfolded as I recalled the scene that John described in his vision of God upon His throne of judgment:

> *Then I saw a great white throne and Him who sat on it, from whose presence earth and heaven fled away, and no place was found for them. And I saw the dead, the great and the small, standing before the throne, and books were opened; and another book was opened, which is the book of life; and the dead were judged from the things which were written in the books, according to their deeds. And the sea gave up the dead which were in it, and death and Hades gave up the dead which were in them; and they were judged, every one of them according to their deeds. Then death and Hades were thrown into the lake of fire. This is the second death, the lake of fire. And if anyone's name was not found written in the book of life, he was thrown into the lake of fire.* (Revelation 20:11–15)

With a resolve to live a better life, I thought, *"The fear of the Lord is the beginning of wisdom!"* (Proverbs 9:10).

Jesus' probing eyes were unflinching. I mustered the courage to speak, "You are worthy to judge all mankind, Lord. Your judgment is just and true.

> There is accountability in God's kingdom.

"There is accountability in Your kingdom, Jesus. All who enter are required to walk worthy of You. Help me to live a life that pleases You." I appealed, realizing the weakness of my flesh.

"Resurrection and eternal judgment are soon to be fully released," He said. "Some have already passed into eternal life. They are the first fruits. But soon all mankind will walk this way. Every person will stand before Me to be judged." (See 1 Corinthians 15:20–23.)

## The Keys of Fire

Jesus stood at the end of the path, staring through the narrow passage toward the beach with a longing like that of a father waiting for a lost child to come home.

I trembled with a sudden chill in the spent afternoon air. Night was approaching quickly, and the rays of light filtering through the narrow passageway were diminishing. In the encroaching darkness, my attention was drawn to the keys chiseled into each stone along the pathway. They were glowing! Each one shone with a luminescent golden-yellow flame. Like the approach lights on an airport runway, they clearly illuminated the pathway into God's kingdom.

I hurriedly turned to get another glimpse of the architectural blueprints before the light faded completely. This time I noticed something very special. Miniature tongues of fire danced upon each page over the symbolic keys.

"They really are supernatural keys, Lord," I said in wonder.

"Yes," He replied. "The Holy Spirit will activate each key in the lives of those who earnestly pursue My kingdom. Human intellect or reason cannot open the way; these are experiential keys."

## My Own Personal Path

I felt a sudden urge to reach into my leather pouch to search the book of symbols. To my delight, Jesus' initials appeared next to every key.

I stared in amazement at the codebook of supernatural symbols. My own spiritual journey unfolded before me. Each personal experience in the Lord was vivid: my deep sorrow and repentance from sin, my acceptance of Jesus as my Savior, my faith in His cleansing blood and mercy as a teenager. The crystal-clear memory of my baptism in water as a believer in a friend's swimming pool seemed like it happened just yesterday. The face of the precious Catholic sister who laid her hands upon me and prayed for me to receive the baptism in the Holy Spirit appeared like a photograph in my mind. The powerful words of prophets and pastors and the laying on of hands of the presbytery as I was ordained into the ministry resounded in my spirit, once again clarifying and confirming my calling and assignment in His kingdom.

"This is my path, Lord," I said, joy bubbling up in my spirit. "This is my experience!"

"That's why I have initialed the symbols," He replied with emphatic approval.

## The Living Way

"The enemy offers an easier way, but its end is destruction," Jesus continued. "Many choose it. But the way that leads to life is narrow, and only a few ever find it. It begins here at this narrow passageway leading into My kingdom. (See Matthew 7:13–14.)

"Listen carefully. I am the Way. No one can come to the Father except through Me. I'm the one who grants a place of repentance to all men; I am the source of faith. You are baptized into Me. I'm the one who baptizes in the Holy Spirit. I am the Resurrection and the Life. I'm the God who judges. I am the pathway into the kingdom. My flesh is the doorway. If anyone enters by Me, he will be saved." (See John 10:9; 14:6.)

## The Second Surveyor's Pin

Mauve-colored clouds hung motionless in the bronze sky as the sun painted one last blazing tapestry of the day's end before its final, smoldering glow would vanish in the darkness of the night.

"We must finish our work," Jesus said.

His words surprised me. I assumed that we had completed the pathway.

He quickly picked up the leather surveyor's bag and the golden hammer and stepped to the very end of the path. Hastily placing my codebook back into my pouch, I hurried to His side.

Jesus opened the bag and withdrew the appropriate surveyor's stake. Handing me the golden hammer, He positioned the pin at the furthest end of the stone of judgment, resting its point in the exact center of the pathway.

The surveyor's marker was solid gold, like the first one, but that's where the similarity ended. This pin had six sides, each one engraved with the name of a specific stone located along the pathway: Repentance, Faith, Baptisms, Laying on of Hands, Resurrection, and Eternal Judgment.

Jesus grasped the marker firmly in both hands. His image, as it was reflected in the six mirror-like faces of the glistening pin, became a visible representation of His provision. It was a perfect symbol of Jesus' life and ministry.

"Drive the pin here, Son!" He commanded.

I struck the surveyor's pin squarely, and it sank comfortably into the soil of the kingdom. In that instant the stones along the pathway drew together, forming one seamless path, one solid rock encompassing the plurality of all the individual stones.

"This is *the* foundation stone of the church," Jesus announced, as He stood to examine the finished work. *"The stone which the builders rejected has become the chief cornerstone"*(Psalm 118:22).

This is *the* foundation stone of the church, the cornerstone.

Paul's words flashed into my mind: *"For no man can lay a foundation other than the one which is laid, which is Jesus Christ"* (1 Corinthians 3:11).

I glanced down at the newly driven surveyor's stake at my feet. It looked like a golden torch ablaze with tongues of fire. A golden crown encircled the base of the shimmering flames, which danced and leaped from a single master key in the center.

## Celestial Sentries

"No one may pass beyond this surveyor's pin unless I grant him permission," the Lord decreed.

He immediately assigned a guard to each side of the path, ordering two of my angelic companions to keep watch. "Allow no one to pass this point until I give them permission," He instructed.

The angels took their positions, standing on respective sides of the pathway with the blazing surveyor's stake between them, celestial sentries on guard duty by command of the Lord of the kingdom. They reminded me of the cherubim God stationed to guard the Garden of Eden, and especially the way to the Tree of Life, after the Fall. (See Genesis 3:24.) The surveyor's pin stood at the center as a clear signal, a spiritual stop sign to all who might try to enter into the kingdom prematurely. No one who lacked a proper foundation would be allowed to proceed.

## No One Sneaks In

Be sure this foundation is laid in the life of every believer you minister to.

Jesus looked back through the passageway and said with a sense of completion, "You must insure that all who approach My kingdom enter through this pathway. Some may try to sneak in another way, but they will be quickly discovered and exposed. Be sure this foundation is laid in the life of every believer you minister to."

Jesus moved toward the beach. I watched His departure, my heart bursting with a sense of gratitude and joy. He was one with the pathway, a part of the seamless stone itself. And then He disappeared from sight.

I hurried through the narrow passageway to the beach and retraced my footsteps along the cliff back to the boat. My angel companion followed at a respectful distance. We sat together on the blanket by the sea, squinting at the architectural drawings as the last glimmer of light was fading away.

The second surveyor's pin was drawn in splendid detail. Jesus' name appeared on each face at the very top. Unfamiliar symbols followed, but to me they seemed similar to Arabic lettering. I couldn't understand them, but I guessed that they might be names—individuals who had a part in the history of the keys, perhaps?

At long last, bone-tired and unable to study any more, I placed the drawings back into the chest and closed it. The angel moved closer to the sacred container and stood at watchful ease. A warm evening breeze gently washed over me, and the sound of the surf played in the stillness of the night. I sat near the entrance to the kingdom of God with peace in my heart.

*Today was incredible,* I thought as my eyes involuntarily closed. *How will I ever explain what I have experienced in His presence to others? They'll never believe such an unusual vision.* Then the Spirit directed my last waking thoughts to the obvious explanation in God's Word:

> *For though by this time you ought to be teachers, you have need again for someone to teach you the elementary principles of the oracles of God, and you have come to need milk and not solid food. For everyone who partakes only of milk is not accustomed to the word of righteousness, for he is an infant. But solid food is for the mature, who because of practice have their senses trained to discern good and evil. Therefore leaving the elementary teaching about the Christ, let us press on to*

*maturity, not laying again a foundation of repentance from dead works and of faith toward God, of instruction about washings and laying on of hands, and the resurrection of the dead and eternal judgment. And this we will do, if God permits.*     (Hebrews 5:12–6:3)

"If God permits," I muttered. "If God permits?" I repeated, a question rather than a statement. "No one can pass into God's kingdom without His permission. And for certain, He'll not grant it until we have proceeded along the narrow pathway that lays His foundation in our lives."

The vision faded, and I found myself back at the well of His presence. I closed my journal and bowed my head in thanksgiving. I had spent an entire day with Him.

## Do You Know Your Assignment?

Some life-changing questions are posed by this vision, which challenge all of us to evaluate our relationship to Jesus. Where are you today in your spiritual journey? Have you proceeded from salvation to His lordship? Are you certain of your calling and the assignment that Christ has given you? Has he granted you permission to proceed into spiritual maturity and fruitfulness?

> As a servant of the Lord Jesus Christ, you are entitled to know your duties.

There are many privileges a servant enjoys, but the only right that a bondslave may demand of his sovereign is to know his master's will. As a servant of the Lord Jesus Christ, you are entitled to know your duties. The Holy Spirit can and will speak to you. Ask Him. His anointed leaders can confirm the things that God whispers to you in the intimacy of the secret place through the Word, prophecy, and counsel.

The Bible is full of examples of individuals who laid their hands on others to impart spiritual gifting and anointing.

Paul wrote to his Christian brothers and sisters in Rome, *"For I long to see you so that I may impart some spiritual gift to you, that you may be established"* (Romans 1:11). God's gifts and callings can, and should be, operating in your life.

The resurrection of the dead and eternal judgment are a constant reminder that we live in a supernatural kingdom where accountability is demanded and required of us. What a glorious privilege and honor it is to serve Jesus Christ, the risen Lord. You should be living with the abiding hope of eternal life and the assurance of God's justice being carried out at the end of the age.

> What a glorious privilege and honor it is to serve Jesus Christ, the risen Lord!

What wonderful discoveries await us! What incredible opportunities stand open before us! We are kingdom saints, and our passion is to pursue His presence, power, and purpose.

May our prayer be, "Lord, grant us Your permission to proceed into the kingdom." And may we hear His reply, "Permission granted."

chapter thirteen

# The King's Scepter

————◆◆◆◆————

Spring finally arrived with its delightful cacophony of
sound and brilliant display of audacious color. The resurrected lawn bristled with impudent violets. Yellow
dandelions arrogantly congregated on the green landscape
like hippies attending a rock concert. Whistling robins
chirped away while a pair of cardinals fed on the abundance
of the new spring growth like lovebirds enraptured with the
joy of togetherness, fearlessly displaying their red plumage.
A mockingbird unapologetically mimicked all of his relatives
from a perch high up in a cedar tree, obviously fancying
himself to be the star of the show.

*How glorious the Garden of Eden must have been,* I
thought as I bowed my head to pray. "Lord, I'm here to walk
with You again just as Enoch walked with You. I love You so
much. Teach me Your ways, Jesus. Show me Your kingdom.
Reveal Yourself to me. You are my life, my joy."

## The Vision Continues

I waited quietly for a moment, basking in the peace of
His presence. And then the still, small voice of the Lord whispered into my spirit. I recorded His words in my journal, just

as I had done for months as He continued to unfold the mysteries of His kingdom.

"Son, I've been waiting for you," He said. "Don't let the circumstances that demand your time call you away from Me. I must show you My kingdom. There is much to do, and there will be plenty of time for you to be refreshed in the midst of this season of revelation. Gather your things, and bring the wicker basket. We will need it today!"

The vision unfolded. We were standing beside the boat on the beach bordering the kingdom of God. My sword was fastened securely to my side, and the leather pouch containing the precious gifts that Jesus gave me for the journey hung comfortably at my waist.

"I'm ready, Lord," I said with eager enthusiasm, reaching into the boat for the wicker basket. When I turned back toward Him, He had already begun to walk up the beach.

We made our way past the first surveyor's pin of the kingdom. It remained exactly where we had driven it. Sparkling in the morning sunlight, the diamond crown cast shimmering beams of brilliance out across the water and wonderful hues of color into the kingdom.

## Permission Granted

We turned into the narrow passage leading toward the kingdom. The early morning air captured inside the sheer cliff walls felt cool and invigorating. *One stone with many faces,* I thought, staring at the supernatural pathway.

When we came to the middle of the narrow gorge, I was expecting a watery passage. To my surprise, I did not sink into the shallow pool. The water supported my weight, and I walked effortlessly across the surface. A fresh wind blew all around us as the Holy Spirit graced our passing with supernatural anointing.

*Of course*, I realized with renewed zeal, *I need a fresh infilling of His Spirit every day.* I felt recharged, empowered by the life of the Lord. (See Acts 13:52.)

"What a wonderful morning," I said, looking up from the pathway. "I love my life, Lord! How exciting to be a part of Your plans and purposes! Life is so precious."

Jesus stopped so abruptly at the second surveyor's pin that I ran into Him with the wicker basket. He turned to me and smiled. With a gracious wave of His arm, He swept His hand past the pin toward the interior of the kingdom.

> "Permission granted, Friend. You may advance into the kingdom."

"You may proceed," He said. "The foundation has been laid well." The angels nodded their heads when I stepped past the marker. I heard the words of an official-sounding salutation: "Permission granted, Friend. You may advance."

Enthralled with the anticipation of the discoveries ahead of me in the hidden kingdom, my voice quivered as I spoke. "I'm so excited that You've brought me here," I said. "And humbled too, Lord."

## Can You Keep a Secret?

"Son," He responded, "the things that I'm about to show you must not be shared with others until the right time. People will not understand. They need to see the entire picture, not just parts and pieces of this revelation. They might be tempted to live with partial truth, and much harm could be done in the kingdom."

His words of instruction reminded me of the warning that He gave to Peter, James, and John as they came down from the mountain of transfiguration. Jesus said, *"Tell the vision to no one until the Son of Man has risen from the dead"* (Matthew 17:9).

Sudden conviction filled my heart. *How often I've been tempted to prematurely share with others the things that God has spoken to me,* I confessed silently, regretting the occasions when I impulsively revealed things that He gave me in the secret place.

One of the most difficult disciplines to learn is keeping confidentiality when God speaks to us in the secret place. Our human tendency is to rush from His presence and hastily shout to the world what He has revealed. There's a subtle spiritual pride that motivates us to show off before our brothers and sisters in the Lord, a "look-what-God-told-me" attitude that smacks of self-importance.

> One of the most difficult disciplines to learn is keeping confidentiality when God speaks to us in the secret place.

More often than not, what God speaks to us in the intimacy of the secret place is sacred and private. It's like the conversation between lovers, meant for the bedchamber, not for the streets. Some things that are heard in the secret place should be kept secret!

"Lord," I said, my voice cracking, "it's so hard not to tell others what You're showing me. I'm so overwhelmed with the revelation of Your kingdom. Please help me not to share Your mysteries before it's time."

"You will know when you are bordering on disobedience," He replied. "I will speak to you through My Spirit. The appropriate time will come for this vision to be revealed. Be patient until the fullness of what I am releasing is birthed within you."

I knew that I had already crossed over the line, sharing prematurely with a few individuals what God intended to be kept in confidence. "Lord, I will obey the voice of Your Spirit," I determined.

## Construction Zone Ahead

I stepped into the vastness of the kingdom, marshaling every ounce of spiritual sensitivity I possessed. The angel, following close behind me, shifted his weight, adjusting his grasp on the chest of architectural drawings. I hugged the wicker basket with both arms. *It seems a bit heavier now that we've started up this incline,* I thought.

The sound of the distant waves filtering through the narrow entrance to the kingdom diminished gradually and then fell silent. I scoured the landscape, not wanting to miss a single thing. The pathway widened as we proceeded inland. I was surprised when I heard the unexpected sounds of construction coming from just beyond the approaching hilltop.

The moment we reached the crest of the hill, a perfectly designed suburban area came into view. The streets were carefully laid out. Houses in various stages of construction lined them. Everything was very orderly. All types of workers were hustling about, skillfully attending to their tasks; some were constructing foundations, others framing and roofing. An entire team of workers attended to each dwelling.

## Kingdom Builders

"What does this mean, Lord?" I asked, knowing that God speaks in symbolic language.

"This process is continually going on in My kingdom," He explained. "I'm building My church. I build it individual by individual. Each house that you see here represents the life of a person, a precious treasure to Me. No two are identical.

> "Each house you see here represents the life of a person, a precious treasure to Me."

"There are similarities, though," He continued, "and those who find that they have the same calling often connect with others of like spirit and gifting.

This helps them to fulfill their destiny. Nonetheless, I have chosen to build My church stone by stone."

The Lord surveyed the process with a discerning eye. It was obvious that He loved each worker and every person that each house symbolized.

The sound of voices drew my attention back to the narrow entrance into the kingdom. To my delight, a steady stream of individuals coming from the world filed past the second surveyor's pin into the kingdom. Workers were greeting the new arrivals and giving directions. I could see more laborers moving toward the entrance from within the kingdom. They clustered in small groups to talk and pray with the new disciples. Eventually, they moved off together to begin the construction of more houses.

## The King's Apprentices

"Lord, what's happening here?" I asked.

"My evangelists and witnesses are constantly pointing people toward Me and ushering them up the narrow pathway into My kingdom," He answered.

"Those who embrace My lordship are given an assignment. My prophets and apostles help them to get established in the church. I provide compassionate care through My pastors, who express My love and concern to them. This is how they grow and mature in their faith and walk." (See 1 Peter 5:1–5.)

*Thank God for anointed ministers,* I thought as I watched the continuing stream of new arrivals from my vantage point on the hillside. Joy graced each face. Every individual was lovingly cared for and given clear oversight and direction. The entire scene was one of great peace and order.

"This is Your kingdom in operation," I observed, overwhelmed by what I saw. "I'm so blessed to be a part of it."

## Raising Spiritual Daughters and Sons

"There is a secret to the process of spiritual growth that you're observing," Jesus said, motioning for me to follow Him into the city.

"My children are a reflection of Me," He explained with a fatherly tone. "It's crucial that they be raised according to My standards. I want them to reflect My nature and personality."

> God's children are a reflection of Jesus, of His nature and personality.

We passed through the streets of the kingdom, traversing several distinct communities. I marveled at the wonderful variety of homes along the streets. We continued for some time, eventually turning onto a wide avenue, which led into a large open plaza. I could see in the distance that a great crowd had assembled in the park. It was evident that they were eagerly anticipating our arrival.

"They're coming!" someone yelled. "I see Him!" someone else shouted. An excited roar went through the gathering as we approached. Shouts of exuberant praise greeted us. Every eye focused on Jesus. His hand intentionally grazed across the leather surveyor's bag at His side, then He glanced at me to see if I noticed.

*What's He up to?* I wondered.

Surrounded and jostled by the jubilant throng, Jesus motioned for everyone to be seated. A hushed stillness ensued. He slowly looked around at the congregation of women, men, and young people. No one seemed to care that He took so much time. Every person enjoyed a singular moment of intimacy with Him. It was obvious that He knew each one. A smile graced His face when He made eye contact with certain individuals.

*No doubt an acknowledgment of shared memories and intimate fellowship,* I thought.

And then He turned in my direction.

*He's looking at me!*

For an instant—or was it for hours—I was alone with Him, in His presence, in the secret place.

## Kingdom Mealtime

He spoke to the assembly for several hours. At times He wept with tender compassion, and then He would laugh with unabashed joy. My eyes were transfixed on Him. His words were life-giving. A hushed awe filled the plaza as we listened with rapt attention. No one wanted to miss a single word.

His words are life-giving.

It wasn't long until it became obvious to me that everyone in this family gathering was personally invited. We were summoned to appear before Jesus. Many came at great sacrifice, and it was evident that they were totally committed to Him.

Jesus turned to look at me. "Bring the basket, Son!" He commanded.

I jumped up and obediently placed the wicker basket at His feet in the center of the assembly. He lifted the loaf of bread and the bottle of wine from inside the simple container and lifted them up toward heaven.

He said, "Father..."

The holiness of God settled over the congregation like a glistening white garment let down from heaven. No one spoke. Many wept.

After choosing a few people to serve, Jesus instructed them to distribute the bread and wine throughout the assembly.

We ate and drank in His presence.

When everyone was finished, He placed the remaining bread and wine back in the basket, closed it, and set it to one side.

"Unless you eat of My flesh and drink of My blood, you have no part with Me!" He declared. "Do this often so you will never forget!" (See John 6:53; 1 Corinthians 11:24–25.)

## The Kingdom Question

For a long time, we sat in His presence, heads bowed in reverence, weeping in gratitude or praying softly. Then He called a single individual out of the crowd, inviting him by name to come closer. I watched attentively.

Jesus did not hurry, taking all the time needed to minister to each concern raised by the apprehensive man. Questions were asked and answered. Jesus would nod His head and gesture yes or no in response. The dialogue was intimate and personal. At the end of the conversation, Jesus asked him a pointed question: "Do you love Me?"

The affirmative response resulted in a powerful declaration: "Feed My sheep and tend My lambs!" (See John 21:15–19.)

## The Soil of the Heart

Then the most amazing thing happened. I watched in astonishment as Jesus reached into the surveyor's bag and withdrew the third surveyor's pin. The gold object was resplendent. It gleamed with regal authority. It was strikingly different from the first two. To my surprise, it had no point; the bottom was perfectly flat.

"How can He drive this stake into the soil?" I wondered in dismay. The mystery was quickly solved.

Jesus took the supernatural surveyor's pin and held it gently against the man's chest. His hand radiated light as the golden stake rested over the pulsing human heart. Something supernatural was taking place. I stared transfixed as the man's appearance changed. A spirit of humility came upon this servant of God. When Jesus finally withdrew the pin, it was obvious that the man was transformed.

## The Third Surveyor's Pin

*This pin must have great power,* I thought, turning to consult the architectural drawings. I shivered with excitement; the zeal to discover God's ways consumed me.

The five adjoining faces of the hollow pin were individually displayed, much like a map of the world when it is spread out on a flat sheet so that the entire landmass can be seen. Each face was identified by a single title: Apostle, Prophet, Evangelist, Pastor, and Teacher.

"The five-fold ministry!" I declared.

Paul's words flashed into my mind:

*But to each one of us grace was given according to the measure of Christ's gift. Therefore He says: "When He ascended on high, He led captivity captive, and gave gifts to men.",...And He Himself gave some to be apostles, some prophets, some evangelists, and some pastors and teachers, for the equipping of the saints for the work of ministry, for the edifying of the body of Christ.*
(Ephesians 4:7–8, 11–12 NKJV)

The top of the pin consisted of five triangular segments. They rose to a cone-shaped point. Each gleaming facet was highly polished silver. This crown kept the five sides in place. Like five facets of a single diamond, each segment revealed an aspect of Jesus' ministry. This supernatural capstone represented the fullness of Christ in the church.

## The Shepherd's Rod and Staff

*This is more than a surveyor's stake!* I thought. *This pin resonates with regal authority. Perhaps it's a rod or a staff. No, that's not adequate to describe its importance.*

"This is the royal scepter of the King of Kings!" I declared with highest regard.

I looked carefully at the Draftsman's notations. They revealed that the inside surface of each side was made out of different material from the others. Each unique element represented the different abilities, characteristics, and qualities of that particular ministry.

"Now I understand!" I blurted out, a flash of insight quickening my spirit. I jumped back and handed the drawings to the angel.

"It makes perfect sense why Jesus held this scepter over the man's chest. The King of Kings sets this surveyor's pin into the heart of every apostle, prophet, evangelist, pastor, and teacher.

> The King of Kings sets this pin into the heart of every apostle, prophet, evangelist, pastor, and teacher.

"Praise God!" I shouted with the joy of newly discovered revelation. "These drawings are spiritual. This third surveyor's pin isn't made of precious metal or valuable gemstones at all. It's made of flesh and blood, actual apostles, prophets, evangelists, pastors, and teachers themselves. They *are* the surveyor's stake," I exclaimed. "They are living epistles, given for all to see. They reflect the Lord of the kingdom. They *are* His representatives, the hand of Jesus at work in building His church." (See 2 Corinthians 3:2–3 NKJV.)

I turned toward the Lord, the architectural drawings still fresh in my mind. "You've learned well, Son," He declared with the approval of a teacher who knows that his student understands the lesson. "No one can build My church unless My government is firmly established in his heart. Those whom I release into five-fold ministry represent My authority. I have given them the necessary insight needed for their part in the work. Only those I call and commission are able to function in this capacity. (See 1 Corinthians 3:9–11.)

"Everyone who receives them will mature and, in turn, will be released into service in My kingdom. In the days to come, it is essential that My people learn to respect these individuals and embrace their ministry. (See Matthew 10:41.)

## Discerning Kingdom Quality

A sudden, sobering wind blew across my spirit. The Lord's voice shook me to my toes. A terrible warning checked my enthusiasm.

> Examine ministers' fruit to see if what they claim is truly established in their hearts.

"All who encounter these kingdom ministries must discern their authenticity," Jesus said. "Tell My children to use wisdom. The enemy counterfeits My gifts and callings. There are false apostles and prophets. Examine their fruit to see if what they claim is truly established in their hearts. One sure sign of genuineness is a willingness to endure hardship, suffering, and even martyrdom for My sake and the sake of the kingdom.

"Tell them to look for the surveyor's stake in the hearts of those who claim to be My servants. My presence will shine through them. When you can see My face, touch My heart, and sense My love, then you'll know that that person is a genuine servant of Mine. But if you observe self-interest, self-promotion, and personal ambition, you should be on guard. Striving and kingdom building, which honors man and not Me, is a clear indication of falsehood and ungodly motives. Do not receive those who do such things. [1]

"I'm not building an organization or seeking to establish a doctrine," Jesus emphasized. "I do not build personality cults! I am building one thing and only one thing—My church. I am establishing My kingdom. Only that which glorifies Me will survive the shaking that is coming upon the earth." (See 1 Corinthians 1:10–17.)

His words brought to mind the ominous warning of the New Testament.

*See to it that you do not refuse Him who is speaking.
For if those did not escape when they refused him who
warned them on earth, much less will we escape who
turn away from Him who warns from heaven. And
His voice shook the earth then, but now He has promised, saying, "YET ONCE MORE I WILL SHAKE NOT ONLY
THE EARTH, BUT ALSO THE HEAVEN." This expression, "Yet
once more," denotes the removing of those things which
can be shaken, as of created things, so that those things
which cannot be shaken may remain. Therefore, since
we receive a kingdom which cannot be shaken, let us
show gratitude, by which we may offer to God an
acceptable service with reverence and awe; for our God
is a consuming fire.* (Hebrews 12:25–29)

## The Commissions Continue

I watched the intimate process continue. Jesus called
each individual from the crowd. Some looked directly into
His eyes or touched His hands. Several knelt at His feet
with their heads bowed, carefully listening to every word of
instruction. A few He tenderly held in His arms. I was moved
to tears.

When He was finished, Jesus placed the surveyor's pin
back into the leather bag, but I knew He would use it again
in the future to impart His anointing and authority to others
still waiting for the call.

## Touching the Father's Heart

Jesus dismissed the crowd, and people quickly dispersed
in every direction. Everyone moved with fresh purpose and
resolution. Some headed toward the entrance to the kingdom. Others filtered into the streets of the city, heading for
specific houses or toward undeveloped land that needed to
be prepared for the construction of new homes. Many carried
scrolls and books for study and reference.

I sat, lost in thought, pondering this incredible experience. Almost everyone had gone when I was startled by the sound of my name. "Dale, come here," Jesus called out to me as He opened the leather bag. "I want you to touch the pin."

I reached into the leather case, my eyes studying the Lord's face for any clue of why He had granted this undeserved favor. I gently grasped the surveyor's stake.

"It's beating!" I gasped, stiffening in shocked surprise. The surveyor's pin was pulsating like a human heart.

"Those who touch this pin touch My heart," Jesus whispered. "They enter into intimacy with Me. I am willing to share My deepest desires with them. That's why they can build My church; they know My heart.

> Jesus is willing to share the deepest desires of His heart with anyone who enters into intimacy with Him.

"They are gifts for My bride," He smiled. "Foundation layers, master builders, My prophetic voice, My wisdom and understanding made plain, My compassion for the lost and dying," He explained, pausing between each for emphasis.

He grasped the cover on the leather case, and I withdrew my hand from the bag. *I must stay close to His heartbeat,* I resolved. *This is the only way to serve and represent Him.*

## Prayer Cover

The plaza was deserted. The wicker basket lay nearby on the lawn. Jesus moved to the far side of the park and knelt in solitude beneath the leafy canopy of a massive oak tree to pray. An expression of great concern covered His face.

*He's interceding for those He's just commissioned,* I discerned. Long pauses interrupted His prayer as He listened to the Father's replies. From time to time, He would smile with a tenderheartedness that reassured me. *None of His servants are without the covering of His prayers!* I thought, relieved to know that He shepherds His flock.

I sat down on the soft grass to reflect upon the events of the day. Once again, Paul's words surfaced in my thoughts:

*And He gave some as apostles, and some as prophets, and some as evangelists, and some as pastors and teachers, for the equipping of the saints for the work of service, to the building up of the body of Christ; until we all attain to the unity of the faith, and of the knowledge of the Son of God, to a mature man, to the measure of the stature which belongs to the fullness of Christ. As a result, we are no longer to be children, tossed here and there by waves and carried about by every wind of doctrine, by the trickery of men, by craftiness in deceitful scheming; but speaking the truth in love, we are to grow up in all aspects into Him who is the head, even Christ, from whom the whole body, being fitted and held together by what every joint supplies, according to the proper working of each individual part, causes the growth of the body for the building up of itself in love.*

(Ephesians 4:11–16)

## It's Time to Grow Up

Every one of God's children has a ministry, but some are called to special duty as His gift to the church. Their assignment is to equip us for the work of the ministry. They are spiritual mothers and fathers; they help the church to mature. How we receive them will determine the extent to which we profit from their ministry.

> Every one of God's children has a ministry, but some are called to special duty as His gift to the church.

209

Jesus is the only true standard of spiritual maturity. We should never gauge our growth or maturity by any other measurement. We certainly shouldn't compare ourselves with each other.

We are to attain to nothing less than the stature and fullness of Christ. Then and only then will His kingdom be demonstrated on earth in awesome power. God's will is that we be joined in perfect unity as His body. (See Ephesians 4:13; John 17:11, 21.)

> It's time for all of us to grow up!

"It's time for all of us to grow up!" I called across the empty plaza. "It'll take a real miracle, Jesus; but with You, Lord, nothing is impossible. You said so Yourself."

*I must get back to the boat,* I thought, despite my reluctance to leave His presence. *The world must know about this amazing place.*

The vision faded. I scanned the filled pages of my journal in amazement. *Every word and paragraph, it's all been written here in the secret place,* I sighed. *It's all here! This revelation, drawn from the well of His presence, is a glimpse into the hidden kingdom.*

"I must return tomorrow," I vowed. "The journey must be completed."

chapter fourteen

# Kingdom Reflections

---◆◆◆◆◆---

The pulsating "whoosh, whoosh" grew steadily louder as the sound of the waves surged through the narrow fissure. I ran, hurrying down the kingdom hillside, back toward the entrance and the open sea beyond. *The wind has risen*, I thought, tugging at my loose collar to ward off the bracing chill of midnight.

I slowed to a respectful walk, panting to catch my breath, and then stepped cautiously past the angel sentries into the narrow passageway. The flickering torchlight radiating from the surveyor's pin behind me cast my shadow upon the vertical stone walls, sending two of me dancing down the cliff face. The twin mimes exaggerated my every move. Far above, a narrow strip of stars twinkled in the black sky like fiber-optic diamonds framed between the parallel edges of the cliff tops.

Refreshing warmth blew into the passageway from the approaching entrance. "Only a few more paces and I'll be on the beach," I whispered into the darkness. I stepped from the secret entrance onto the soft granular sand of the beach. Iridescent particles of brilliance showered from the face of the ice-blue sapphire on the first surveyor's pin. White-hot droplets of light splashed over my feet and flickered like a Fourth of July sparkler as I passed by.

The subdued whooshing sound that I first noticed back in the kingdom now resonated like the thunder of timpani drums. Each successive wave built up to a height of several feet offshore and then crashed near the shore with incredible force.

With a constancy like that of a skilled percussion section in a world-class symphony orchestra, each wave rose, held its place, and then broke on command, as if it were responding to an invisible conductor. My chest vibrated in response. Captivated by this power and rhythm, I made my way along the beach toward the boat with a sense of wonder, unable to keep my eyes off the pounding surf.

## Written on the Waves

*It'll be hours before daybreak,* I thought. *I might as well sit here in the boat until dawn.* The small vessel creaked and rolled slightly as I placed my weight on the port side and swung one leg into the curved bottom, hoisting myself onto the seat facing the water's expanse.

Instantly, my eyes surveyed an incredible scene. The sea was transformed. I was no longer looking at customary waves rising and crashing in the darkness. To my amazement, words began to appear upon the face of each crest, like white letters scrolling down the black background of a television screen. I watched, transfixed, as each wave brought a new revelation from the Scriptures, a unique aspect of God's kingdom.

Kingdom truth came crashing into my spirit.

"I'm an audience of one!" I uttered with delight, realizing that the Holy Spirit was the conductor and I was the listener. I set myself for the next wave. Kingdom truth came crashing into my spirit.

## The Master's Message

The words that scrolled across the approaching wave provoked an ancient scene in my mind. I could see Jesus standing on the gentle slope of a hillside. The calm, brilliant-blue Sea of Galilee stretched out to the south. A crowd of followers, numbering in the thousands, sat in the heat of the Eastern afternoon sun listening with rapt attention while He spoke.

*Blessed are the poor in spirit, for theirs is the kingdom of heaven....Blessed are those who have been persecuted for the sake of righteousness, for theirs is the kingdom of heaven. Blessed are you when people insult you and persecute you, and falsely say all kinds of evil against you because of Me. Rejoice and be glad, for your reward in heaven is great; for in the same way they persecuted the prophets who were before you.* (Matthew 5:3, 10–12)

*You are the salt of the earth; but if the salt has become tasteless, how can it be made salty again?...You are the light of the world. A city set on a hill cannot be hidden....Let your light shine before men in such a way that they may see your good works, and glorify your Father who is in heaven.* (Matthew 5:13–14, 16)

*Do not think that I came to abolish the Law or the Prophets; I did not come to abolish but to fulfill....Whoever then annuls one of the least of these commandments, and teaches others to do the same, shall be called least in the kingdom of heaven; but whoever keeps and teaches them, he shall be called great in the kingdom of heaven. For I say to you that unless your righteousness surpasses that of the scribes and Pharisees, you will not enter the kingdom of heaven.* (Matthew 5:17, 19–20)

*For this reason I say to you, do not be worried about your life....Look at the birds of the air...the lilies of the field....But seek first the kingdom of God and His righteousness, and all these things will be added unto you.* (Matthew 6:25–26, 28, 33)

*Not everyone who says to me "Lord, Lord," will enter the kingdom of heaven, but he who does the will of My Father who is in heaven will enter....Therefore everyone who hears these words of Mine and acts on them, may be compared to a wise man who built his house upon the rock. And the rain fell, and the floods came, and the winds blew and slammed against that house, and yet it did not fall, for it had been founded on the rock.*
(Matthew 7:21, 24–25)

"The Sermon on the Mount!" I blurted out in astonishment. "It's all here, written in this wave of truth. It's about the kingdom. Jesus was speaking about the kingdom of God!" I exclaimed.

Everything I've learned in years of studying the Sermon on the Mount crystallized into one obvious undeniable theme. I was drenched in this singular truth. "All of the Beatitudes, the instructions about prayer and fasting and giving alms—it's all about God's government in our lives. It is the kingdom revealed," I realized.

## The Kingdom Prayer

The first wave discharged its message, driving it into my spirit with great force. Without pause, the next wave rose behind it to deliver another powerful truth.

*But you, when you pray, go into your room, and when you have shut your door, pray to your Father who is in **the secret place**; and your Father who sees in secret will reward you openly....In this manner, therefore, pray: Our Father in heaven, Hallowed be Your name. **Your kingdom come. Your will be done on earth as it is in heaven**. Give us this day our daily bread. And forgive us our debts, as we forgive our debtors. And do not lead us into temptation, but deliver us from the evil one. For **Yours is the kingdom** and the power and the glory forever. Amen.*
(Matthew 6:6, 9–13 NKJV, emphasis added)

"Yes, that's it! That's what it's all about, Jesus," I announced with fresh conviction. "The rewards of the kingdom are discovered and released in the secret place. That's what You desire. It's not about us; it's about Your will being done here on earth. It's about Your kingdom coming!"

> The rewards of the kingdom are discovered and released in the secret place.

## For Your Eyes Only

I searched the water eagerly, my spiritual hunger increasing with each successive wave of truth. "Teach me more about Your kingdom, Lord," I prayed.

The words shimmered like silver letters, handwritten upon the opaque watery surface. Ancient, yet vibrant with meaning, the Scriptures seemed to come alive. God was speaking to me as though I were the only one listening.

*And the disciples came and said to Him, "Why do You speak to them in parables?" He answered and said to them, "Because it has been given to you to know the mysteries of the kingdom of heaven, but to them it has not been given. For whoever has, to him more will be given, and he will have abundance; but whoever does not have, even what he has will be taken away from him. Therefore I speak to them in parables, because seeing they do not see, and hearing they do not hear, nor do they understand. And in them the prophecy of Isaiah is fulfilled, which says: 'Hearing you will hear and shall not understand, and seeing you will see and not perceive; for the hearts of this people have grown dull. Their ears are hard of hearing, and their eyes they have closed, lest they should see with their eyes and hear with their ears, lest they should understand with their hearts and turn, so that I should heal them.' But blessed are your eyes for they see, and your ears for they*

*hear; for assuredly, I say to you that many prophets and
righteous men desired to see what you see, and did not
see it, and to hear what you hear, and did not hear it."*
(Matthew 13:10–17 NKJV)

"Of course!" I blurted out like a spiritual Sherlock
Holmes. "It's so obvious to the awakened spirit," I acknowledged. "If only everyone could see," I paused with a sudden
pain of sadness.

"But there is hope, Lord," I continued, finally. "You can
open the blinded eyes of those who seek Your truth."

## A Spiritual Treasure Hunt

Jesus taught in parables for a specific reason. His aim was
to perplex rather than to persuade His listeners. He sought
to conceal rather than to reveal. He was hiding something,
sharing His secrets only with those who believed in Him. Yet,
even those closest to Him had to ask what He meant. Matthew's gospel clearly indicates that Jesus said nothing to the
crowds without a parable. (See Matthew 13:34.)

My Sunday school teachers taught me that parables are
earthly stories with a heavenly meaning. They are pictures of
something familiar used to illustrate something unfamiliar in
order to shed light on the unknown. Like a magnifying glass,
which gathers the sun's rays and focuses them upon a single
point, the parables of Jesus focus on a singular overarching
truth; they reveal the character of the kingdom of God.

*To whoever has, more will be given,* I reflected.

"Lord, teach me about Your parables," I prayed, staring
eagerly at the approaching wave. His response was instanta-
neous.

## Kingdom Wages

*For the kingdom of heaven is like a landowner who
went out early in the morning to hire laborers for*

*his vineyard. When he had agreed with the laborers for a denarius for the day, he sent them into his vineyard....When evening came, the owner of the vineyard said to his foreman, "Call the laborers and pay them their wages, beginning with the last group to the first." When those hired about the eleventh hour came, each one received a denarius. When those hired first came, they thought that they would receive more; but each of them also received a denarius. When they received it, they grumbled at the landowner, saying, "These last men have worked only one hour, and you have made them equal to us who have borne the burden and the scorching heat of the day." But he answered and said to one of them, "Friend, I am doing you no wrong; did you not agree with me for a denarius? Take what is yours and go, but I wish to give to this last man the same as to you. Is it not lawful for me to do what I wish with what is my own? Or is your eye envious because I am generous?" So the last shall be first, and the first last.* (Matthew 20:1–2, 8–16)

Another wave crested, reiterating this truth:

*When you are invited by someone to a wedding feast, do not take the place of honor, for someone more distinguished than you may have been invited by him, and he who invited you both will come and say to you, "Give your place to this man," and then in disgrace you proceed to occupy the last place. But when you are invited, go and recline at the last place, so that when the one who has invited you comes, he may say to you, "Friend, move up higher"; then you will have honor in the sight of all who are at the table with you. For everyone who exalts himself will be humbled, and he who humbles himself will be exalted.* (Luke 14:8–11)

"It's so clear, Lord," I realized. "The rewards of the kingdom are not determined by what we think we have earned or deserve, or even by how long we may have served You when compared to others. They are the free gift of Your grace, and You bestow them upon whomever You choose, in the measure that You choose. Seeking the seat of honor will not do. You will simply not tolerate an 'I-deserve-more-than-others' attitude.

> **Rewards in the kingdom are gifts from God. He decides our wages.**

"There are no rights that stem from the responsibilities we fulfill or the assignments we carry out. We should never demand rewards for our kingdom labor, no matter how diligently we have preformed our duties. We can never store up enough merit to put You in our debt. Rewards in the kingdom are gifts from You. You decide our wages."

## Preserving the Kingdom

With relentless persistence, line upon line, precept upon precept, wave upon wave, the Holy Spirit continued to release revelation from the Word.

> *But no one puts a patch of unshrunk cloth on an old garment; for the patch pulls away from the garment, and a worse tear results. Nor do people put new wine into old wineskins; otherwise the wineskins burst, and the wine pours out and the wineskins are ruined; but they put new wine into fresh wineskins, and both are preserved.* (Matthew 9:16–17)

"Lord," I confessed, "this is scary. Are You saying that man's structures and religious institutions cannot serve as the vehicle for Your kingdom? I keep trying to patch up the institution with new cloth. I keep rubbing oil on the wineskin in the hope it will stay pliable.

"You destroy all my altars of stability," I realized, gripping the familiar wooden seat of the boat instinctively. "You change all my definitions. Your kingdom shatters the structures of the old man-made order. Religious institutions and pharisaical self-righteousness cannot contain the new wine of the kingdom. Your kingdom requires pliable, yielded vessels.

> God's kingdom shatters the man-made structures of religious institutions.

"Lord, help me to let go of the old ways and embrace the kingdom. Help me to loosen my grip on self-preservation."

## Tiny Beginnings, Astonishing Endings

In an instant, the Holy Spirit answered my prayer. Self-preservation suddenly seemed trite in comparison to His intentions. God's aim is to bring increase, abundant fruitfulness, and fulfillment. The kingdom is all about incredible, supernatural growth.

> *And He spoke many things to them in parables, saying, "Behold, the sower went out to sow....And the one on whom seed was sown on the good soil, this is the man who hears the word and understands it; who indeed bears fruit and brings forth, some a hundredfold, some sixty, and some thirty."* (Matthew 13:3, 23)

> *Another parable He put forth to them, saying: "The kingdom of heaven is like a mustard seed, which a man took and sowed in his field, which indeed is the least of all the seeds; but when it is grown it is greater than the herbs and becomes a tree, so that the birds of the air come and nest in its branches."* (Matthew 13:31–32 NKJV)

> *He spoke another parable to them, "The kingdom of heaven is like leaven, which a woman took and hid in three pecks of flour until it was all leavened."* (Matthew 13:33)

"God's kingdom is coming!" I stated confidently. "It can't be stopped. There's supernatural power in kingdom seed. It's being planted in the hearts of mankind. It will bring forth an incredible harvest," I said, glancing up from the cresting wave toward the distant dark horizon.

"The seed grows secretly, but watch out: His kingdom is coming. It will eventually fill the earth," I shouted above the crashing noise.

## Warning: Judgment Ahead

A towering wave of revelation rose in front of me, and a shudder of apprehension trickled down my spine. A sense of urgency gripped me as I took in the full impact of the words scrolling across the aqua surface.

> *Behold the fig tree and all the trees; as soon as they put forth leaves, you see it and know for yourselves that summer is now near. So you also, when you see these things happening, recognize that the kingdom of God is near.* (Luke 21:29–31)

"No one knows the day or the hour, Lord," I whispered, "but we're supposed to read the weather signs."

The parable continued to unfold before me, warning of impending judgment and the urgency of watchfulness.

> *But be sure of this, that if the head of the house had known at what time of the night the thief was coming, he would have been on the alert and would not have allowed his house to be broken into. For this reason you also must be ready; for the Son of Man is coming at an hour when you do not think He will.* (Matthew 24:43–44)

> *Then the kingdom of heaven shall be likened to ten virgins who took their lamps and went out to meet the bridegroom. Now five of them were wise, and five were foolish....And while they went to buy, the bridegroom came, and those who were ready went in with him to the wedding; and the door was shut. Afterward the other virgins came also, saying, "Lord, Lord, open to us!" But he answered and said, "Assuredly, I say to you, I do*

*not know you. Watch therefore, for you know neither the day nor the hour in which the Son of Man is coming."*
(Matthew 25:1–2, 10–13 NKJV)

Even Christians can be lulled to sleep. How much God wants to alert us to the coming catastrophe! The world is rushing headlong toward judgment. We need to be shocked awake before it's too late. The King is coming!

## God's Lost and Found Department

The brilliant moonlight filtered through the next wave, filling it with a soft buttery glow. Hope seemed to emanate from the transparent liquid, providing an encouraging context for the unfolding message.

*What man among you, if he has a hundred sheep and has lost one of them, does not leave the ninety-nine in the open pasture and go after the one which is lost until he finds it? When he has found it, he lays it on his shoulders, rejoicing. And when he comes home, he calls together his friends and his neighbors, saying to them, "Rejoice with me, for I have found my sheep which was lost!" I tell you that in the same way, there will be more joy in heaven over one sinner who repents than over ninety-nine righteous persons who need no repentance.*
(Luke 15:4–7)

*Or what woman, if she has ten silver coins and loses one coin, does not light a lamp and sweep the house and search carefully until she finds it? When she has found it, she calls together her friends and neighbors, saying, "Rejoice with me, for I have found the coin which I had lost!" In the same way, I tell you, there is joy in the presence of the angels of God over one sinner who repents.*
(Luke 15:8–10)

*A man had two sons....*                                    (v. 11)

The story continued on. The departed prodigal squandered his inheritance, ending up in the squalor of the pigpen.

Finally, out of desperation, he returned to his father's house.

> *So he got up and came to his father. But while he was still a long way off, his father saw him and felt compassion for him, and ran and embraced him and kissed him.* (Luke 15:20)

The father explained to the chagrined elder brother, *"But we had to celebrate and rejoice, for this brother of yours was dead and has begun to live, and was lost and has been found"* (v. 32). [1]

And still another passage scrolled across the wave:

> *A certain man gave a great supper and invited many, and sent his servant at supper time to say to those who were invited, "Come, for all things are now ready." But they all with one accord began to make excuses....So that servant came and reported these things to his master. Then the master of the house, being angry, said to his servant, "Go out quickly into the streets and lanes of the city, and bring in here the poor and the maimed and the lame and the blind." And the servant said, "Master, it is done as you commanded, and still there is room." Then the master said to the servant, "Go out into the highways and hedges, and compel them to come in, that my house may be filled."* (Luke 14:16–18, 21–23 NKJV)

I heaved a huge sigh. "Father, Your love is limitless," I said. "It makes room for another chance, another opportunity for grace and mercy. No matter how many times we mess up, You watch and wait for us to find our way back home to You. You even continue to seek for those who are lost or have strayed."

There's room in God's kingdom for the imperfect. It's not the healthy but the sick who need a physician, and it's the sinner who needs a Savior. God's kingdom is populated by the broken who have been made whole and failures who have been restored. His kingdom is the lost and found department of the universe, the Adullam's cave of spiritual failures transformed into redeemed warriors. (See 1 Samuel 22:1–2; 23:5.)

> God's kingdom is populated by the broken made whole.

## The Merciful King

"Cleanse my heart from pride and self-importance," I prayed. "Help me not to be offended by the inclusive nature of Your love, Lord. All are welcome in the kingdom. Those who respond to the invitation are received into the banquet hall. Your kingdom is inclusive!

"Whosoever will, may come," I said, with assurance. "Help me to rejoice when it's party time in Your house, Jesus. After all, who am I to judge others? I'm one of the ones that You gave another chance to!" My tears glistened in the moonlight.

## A Priceless Treasure

The next wave drew me in with golden magnetism.

*The kingdom of heaven is like a treasure hidden in the field, which a man found and hid again; and from joy over it he goes and sells all that he has and buys that field. Again, the kingdom of heaven is like a merchant seeking fine pearls, and upon finding one pearl of great value, he went and sold all that he had and bought it.*
(Matthew 13:44–46)

"What could possibly be worth more than Your kingdom, Lord?" I pondered. "It is so priceless that it's worth selling all that we posses to obtain it. Our emphasis shouldn't be on what we have to give up, but rather on what we have found. Your kingdom makes everything else pale in comparison."

## A Dreadful Sound

With a dreadful surge of unleashed agony, the incongruous wave lifted out of the sea, gathering toward the shore with tormented force. Spilling its awfulness, it exploded at the shoreline of the kingdom, a final movement of symphonic pain. Its foul sound drained life from me. Shrieking strings, pounding brass, wailing woodwinds—the ghastly wave of misery fell on the shore of the kingdom, spent, and came crashing to a bitter death, a forever ending—an eternal dissonance, an unforgettable tormenting sound.

I sat terrified in ice-cold clamminess, nauseated by the dreadful message.

> *So it will be at the end of the age....There will be weeping and gnashing of teeth.* (Matthew 13:49–50)

Such horrible words of ultimate doom! The utter pain and hopelessness of this inescapable finale for mankind played out in my horrified imagination. I desperately wanted to put it right, to bring resolution, but I could not!

> *The kingdom of heaven may be compared to a man who sowed good seed in his field. But while his men were sleeping, his enemy came and sowed tares among the wheat, and went away. But when the wheat sprouted and bore grain, then the tares became evident also. The slaves of the landowner came and said to him, "Sir, did you not sow good seed in your field? How then does it have tares?" And he said to them, "An enemy has done this!" The slaves said to him, "Do you want us, then, to go and gather them up?" But he said, "No; for while you are gathering up the tares, you may uproot the wheat with them. Allow both to grow together until the harvest; and in the time of the harvest I will say to the reapers, 'First gather up the tares and bind them in bundles to burn them up; but gather the wheat into my barn.'"* (Matthew 13:24–30)

*Again, the kingdom of heaven is like a dragnet cast into the sea, and gathering fish of every kind; and when it was filled, they drew it up on the beach; and they sat down and gathered the good fish into containers, but the bad they threw away. So it will be at the end of the age; the angels will come forth and take out the wicked from among the righteous, and will throw them into the furnace of fire; in that place there will be weeping and gnashing of teeth.* (Matthew 13:47–50)

The enemy of the kingdom is now at work relentlessly sowing evil. It's often hard for us to distinguish between the genuine and the counterfeit. The final judgment is reserved for God. Our focus and responsibility is to keep sowing "good seed" while there is still time.

> Keep sowing *"good seed"* while there is still time.

## Kingdom Scribes

The sea settled to a silent calm. One final message scrolled across the resting surface: *"Have you understood all these things?"* (Matthew 13:51).

"Yes, Lord," I replied.

Then He said, *"Therefore every scribe who has become a disciple of the kingdom of heaven is like a head of household, who brings out of his treasure things new and old"* (Matthew 13:52).

The ocean lay as smooth as glass, its symphony concluded. I sat alone on the shore of the kingdom, engulfed in the stillness.

chapter fifteen

# The Great Mistake

---◆◆◆◆---

The stars seemed to be frozen in place, captured by the tranquil sea. I gripped the weathered wooden plank of my seat with both hands, not wanting a muscle to even quiver. I inhaled and then paused, holding my breath to capture the tangible essence of the total calm that encompassed me. *It's like the empty void of pre-creation,* I thought, trying not to blink in case I might disturb the stillness. *The Holy Spirit is brooding over the water.*

It was so quiet that I was conscious of the silence. *"Man does not put silence to the test, silence puts man to the test."* [1] *Even my thoughts are too loud! I've got to stop this internal dialogue!* I grimaced, struggling to quiet the conversation going on inside of me.

*Be still my soul,* I commanded. *Something's about to happen!*

Like a focused runner crouching at the starting line, waiting for the sound of the official's gun, I poised my spirit for instant response. My skin tingled with anticipation. Every nerve was alert. I could feel the presence of the Holy Spirit. And then, ever so slightly, almost imperceptibly, a gentle wind like an infant's breath wafted across my neck. "Listen and observe carefully," the Spirit said. "There's something you must understand before you return to the world."

Instantly the scene changed. I was no longer sitting in the rowboat. In the Spirit, I was an observer in the Upper Room with the disciples.

## The Wrong Question

The atmosphere in the room was electrifying. Jesus' presence energized everyone. Hope radiated from the face of each listener. A determined bunch, I could see that they were eager to get going. A young man nearby murmured, "There are cities and towns that haven't heard about His resurrection. We've got to go right now," he insisted. "I can't wait to proclaim this miracle. He's alive; the King is really alive! We must establish His throne over Israel."

Jesus spoke with a tone of restraint in His voice. "You must not leave Jerusalem yet," He said. "Wait here until you receive the promise of the Father. Don't you remember what I told you? John baptized with water, but you will be baptized with the Holy Spirit a few days from now."

> Wait to minister until you receive the promise of the Father.

A murmur went through the assembly as they balked at His instructions. Finally, someone near the back of the crowded room spoke up. Like a news reporter at a high-level briefing with a chief government official, the apostle's words were abrupt and provoking. "Lord, aren't You going to restore the kingdom to Israel now?" he challenged with revolutionary zeal. It was obvious by the nodding of every head that his question reflected the thoughts of the entire group of believers.

Jesus' countenance instantly changed. An expression of disappointment exposed His feelings. "You still don't get it,"

He replied. "That information is top secret! It's not for you to know everything that My Father has planned for the future. Just be aware that there are times ahead when you will see His supernatural intervention in this world. There are moments and seasons when the purposes of heaven will intersect with the events of history. This is entirely in My Father's hands. He is the only one who has the authority to decide when these things will occur. He has kept them secret!"

> There are moments and seasons when the purposes of heaven will intersect with the events of history.

The frustration of His listeners was evident on their faces. Trapped in the realm of human logic and reason, they couldn't make any sense out of what He was saying.

He paused, granting them an encouraging smile. As He looked around the room at each precious follower, He explained, "Don't be confused. Once the Holy Spirit has come upon you, you will be empowered to be My witnesses. Then you will be released to spread the message of My kingdom, not only here in Jerusalem, but in Judea, Samaria, and to the very ends of the earth." (See Acts 1:2–8.)

## Still Confused!

The scene changed. It was a little while later on the Mount of Olives. The same confused bunch of believers stood gazing upward into the sky. He was gone, taken up into the heavens, with a cloud as His chariot. They ached for the establishment of God's kingdom and extrication from the oppressive rule of Rome.

Two men standing beside them in white clothing gave instructions. "Why are you standing here gaping at the empty sky? He will come back from heaven in the same way that He left."

*What are we to do?* they wondered in confusion. Someone suggested that they go back to the Upper Room where they could pray and seek His direction. And so they returned there and waited for the command to go, fully expecting to wrestle the kingdom from Rome and establish Jesus upon the throne. (See Acts 1:9–14.)

## Political, Religious, or Spiritual?

The scene faded. As a pupil in the classroom of the Spirit, I sat quietly, considering the vision and pondering the kingdom of God.

*It's so sad,* I reflected.

Since the beginning of the church, we've made the same tragic mistake of seeking to establish an external form of government called the "kingdom of God." We erroneously perceive an imposed divine dictatorship of sovereign authority that will resolve the injustices of life and history. We imagine God's reign to be a utopia of health, peace, and prosperity that will physically and judicially transform the nations. We still don't get it! We think we can make it happen.

Over two thousand years ago, Jesus' followers cried out, "Hosanna to the King!" when He entered Jerusalem for the Passover. They were looking for a political deliverer. Jesus was tried, convicted, and crucified because of the accusation that He was the King of the Jews. He was a perceived threat to the religious and political establishments.

## Jesus' Solution

Even Jesus' handpicked apostles confused the natural with the spiritual. They asked the wrong question: "Will You establish Your kingdom now?" They wanted Jesus to be a political power broker who would crush every other sovereign authority, especially Rome. Instead, He died and rose again—and promised only one solution, the coming of the Holy Spirit!

It's the same today. Well-meaning disciples of Jesus Christ still seek to impose on the church and on the world a form of government that smacks of political maneuvering for positions of influence, advantage, and power. Titles are sought and revered. The important and the wealthy are treated preferentially.

*Oh, how I hate this shameful behavior,* I thought.

The imposition of politics in an attempt to establish the kingdom must be an abomination to God. The kingdom will never come about by might or power. It will only come by the Holy Spirit!

We haven't changed much since biblical times. We're like the bewitched Galatian Christians, who were deceived. They thought that they could complete in the flesh what God began in the Spirit. (See Galatians 3:1–3.)

## Not of This World

Another vision painted an ancient scene in my mind. The place was Jerusalem; the time, early morning; the setting, the Roman Praetorium. Voices echoed in the torch-lit chamber.

"Are You the King of the Jews?" Pilate asked.

"Are you speaking on your own initiative, or did others tell you this about Me?" Jesus answered.

"Am I a Jew? Your own nation and the chief priests have delivered You to me. What have You done?" Pilate asked, implying confirmed guilt.

"My kingdom is not of this world. If My kingdom were of this world, then My servants would fight so that I would not be handed over to the Jews; but as it is, My kingdom is not from here," Jesus stated, answering Pilate's first question.

"You are a king then?" Pilate retorted.

"You say correctly that I am a king," Jesus replied. "For this cause I was born, and for this cause I have come into the world, that I should bear witness to the truth. Everyone who is of the truth hears My voice."

"What is truth?" Pilate retorted, and he walked out of the hall. (See John 18:33–38.)

The words pierced into my spirit like nails driven into living flesh. *"My kingdom is not of this world....My kingdom is not of this world!"* Louder and louder the hammering truth fixed itself in my mind until I was utterly convinced. (See Ecclesiastes 12:11.)

"Your words are crystal-clear," I said. "Your kingdom does not originate in this world. It's not established by the efforts of man. It is a supernatural kingdom. It is in the Holy Spirit!" (See Romans 14:17.)

## Where Is Your Kingdom, Lord?

God's Word flashed into my mind with staggering clarity:

> *The kingdom of God isn't ushered in with visible signs. You won't be able to say, "It has begun here in this place or there in that part of the country." For the Kingdom of God is within you.* (Luke 17:20–21 TLB)

"That's it!" I declared, confessing the truth. "It's not out there; it's inside us. This is what Jesus meant when He said, 'You must be born of the Spirit.' God's kingdom is Spirit-birthed.

"The kingdom of God is not 'out there' in the hallways of government or the throne rooms of earthly kings. It's not to be found in the marketplace or the institutions of men. It's located within the human spirit. We are 'born' into the kingdom. We are impregnated with spiritual seed, conceived by the Holy Spirit. [2] We are spiritual sons and daughters of the Father, and Jesus is our older brother.

> We are spiritual sons and daughters of the Father, and Jesus is our older brother.

"One person at a time, one soul at a time, one heart at a time—that's how the kingdom of God advances. The good news of God's government is like spiritual leaven slowly infiltrating mankind and filling the earth with the glory of God. No nation, no people group, no earthly kingdom can escape the sovereign lordship of Jesus Christ."

## Bondslaves of the King

*If God's kingdom is within us,* I wondered, *then what does it look like?* Instantly, the first surveyor's pin flashed into my mind.

"It looks like Jesus!" I concluded. "The entire focus of the kingdom is Jesus! His will, His heart, His desires, and His purposes are the only priority."

I was absorbed in the thought of what God's kingdom is like. The mandate of the King is servanthood, not self-importance. The issue is not who is the greatest, but rather who is the least. We are to be servants, followers of Jesus' example, foot-washers who carry a cross of self-denial, motivated by the all-consuming love of Jesus for mankind.

The kingdom of God is about our surrender, not our self-preservation. Self-preservation will keep us from fulfilling the will of God. It's in dying to our own will and desires that we find life in the kingdom. The King of Kings takes up residence within us. We are His to command. When we yield our wills to His, we are set free. Those who seek to preserve their lives will lose them, but those who willingly lay their lives down in His service will find them. (See Matthew 16:25.) The distinct privilege of the

Christian is to become a bondslave of Jesus. (See Titus 1:1; Colossians 4:12.)

## Conflicting Kingdoms

But make no mistake; the enemy has his servants too. Their enslavement is to the bondage of every evil thing; their master's intent is to kill and destroy all who serve the Lord Jesus Christ. There are two spiritual kingdoms, God's and Satan's. There is fully declared war between them, a struggle between the forces of light and darkness.

The entire Bible from Genesis to Revelation is framed in the context of this spiritual conflict. The battle lines are clearly drawn. Spiritual warfare is unavoidable! Despite our desire to live in peace, our archenemy will not leave us alone. Every Christian must be a soldier, a warrior in God's army, and a subject of His kingdom. Our allegiance is to Jesus, our Commander in Chief.

Our warfare is not with flesh and blood. Our wrestling is not with people; it is against principalities and powers in the spiritual realm. We battle for the souls of mankind held captive by Satan. Only spiritual weapons can destroy the enemy's strongholds. But the war is almost over. Our victory is assured. Our orders are to stand in faith with supernatural endurance until He returns. (See Ephesians 6:10–20; 2 Corinthians 10:4–6.)

> As kingdom soldiers, our passion is His presence, our strength is His power, and our goal is the fullfillment of His purposes.

We are soldiers of Christ. Our *passion* is His presence, our *strength* is His power, our *goal* is the fulfillment of His purpose. The nations belong to Him. The government is upon His shoulder. He is the Prince of Peace, but peace will not fully come until He does.

The message we proclaim is His lordship, the good news of God's government within the hearts of men. The banner we carry is the unfurled declaration of an invisible realm. Its emblem is a cross; its awesome power, the Resurrection. Its borders are invisible. *It is a hidden kingdom.*

## The Only Choice

*Have this attitude in yourselves which was also in Christ Jesus, who, although He existed in the form of God, did not regard equality with God a thing to be grasped, but emptied Himself, taking the form of a bond-servant, and being made in the likeness of men. Being found in appearance as a man, He humbled Himself by becoming obedient to the point of death, even death on a cross. For this reason also, God highly exalted Him, and bestowed on Him the name which is above every name, so that at the name of Jesus EVERY KNEE WILL BOW, of those who are in heaven and on earth and under the earth, and that every tongue will confess that Jesus Christ is Lord, to the glory of God the Father.* (Philippians 2:5–11)

This is the only option that God offers. We get to choose when, not if, we will bow our knee in acknowledgment that Jesus Christ is Lord. Will it be now or in eternity? Every knee will bow and every tongue will confess that Jesus Christ is Lord!

Paul's words were etched in my mind: *"For to this end Christ died and lived again, that He might be Lord both of the dead and of the living"* (Romans 14:9).

## It's All Because I Love You!

I stared out into the darkness across the peaceful water. I felt like an explorer who had landed on a surreal shore, caught in a time warp between two worlds. I wanted to stay here forever. There was so much to learn, so much to understand. Thoughts and images of the kingdom swirled in my head. But an irresistible tugging drew my attention out across the sea, beyond the darkness and the night, to the distant invisible coast. Something—no, someone—seemed to be calling me back to the world.

Suddenly, unexpectedly, I felt loved. It swept into me like waves massaging my soul. It was more than emotion or feeling. It was tangible, total love, and it was wonderful! Every tinge of resistance and striving drained out of me. I was at peace.

All my previous concerns about His authority and lordship challenging my wishes and prerogatives dissolved. I breathed a sigh of surrender and came to rest in His loving will. I was important to Him. I was the center of His attention, the apple of His eye, His valuable possession. I was wrapped in His arms, His son! He loved me and accepted me unreservedly. He would never ask me to do something that would result in eternal harm.

*Why am I experiencing this now?* I asked myself, and then it dawned upon me. *The Holy Spirit is teaching me one final lesson. He's showing me that love and authority do not contradict one another. In the kingdom of God, they compliment each other. God's government and authority are an extension of His love. God is love!*

The kingdom of God is a wonderful blessing, not a curse. Jesus' authority in our lives is not harmful, it's beneficial. God sent His Son because He loved us. (See John 3:16.) Like a loving parent, He disciplines us because He loves us. All His commands and instructions are motivated by love. (See Hebrews 12:6.)

> The safest place in all the universe is in God's kingdom!

Then the Spirit whispered into my thoughts, "Tell them I love them. Tell those who are reading this at this very moment. Tell them now! Tell them not to fear My authority. Tell them that the safest place in all the universe is in My kingdom!"

## The Same Message from Paul's Pen

The apostle Paul penned these words from Corinth around A.D. 56. They were intended for the Christians in Rome and for us in His kingdom today:

> For from the very beginning God decided that those who came to him—and all along he knew who would— should become like his Son, so that his Son would be the First, with many brothers. And having chosen us, he called us to come to him; and when we came, he declared us "not guilty," filled us with Christ's goodness, gave us right standing with himself, and promised us his glory. What can we ever say to such wonderful things as these? If God is on our side, who can ever be against us? Since he did not spare even his own Son for us but gave him up for us all, won't he also surely give us everything else? Who dares accuse us whom God has chosen for his own? Will God? No! He is the one who has forgiven us and given us right standing with himself. Who then will condemn us? Will Christ? No! For he is the one who died for us and came back to life again for us and is sitting at the place of highest honor next to God, pleading for us there in heaven. Who then can ever keep Christ's love from us? When we have trouble or calamity, when we are hunted down or destroyed, is it because he doesn't love us anymore? And if we are hungry or penniless or in danger or threatened with death, has God deserted us? No, for the Scriptures tell us that for his sake we must be ready to face death at every moment of the day—we are like sheep awaiting slaughter; but despite all this, overwhelming victory is ours through Christ who loved us enough to die for us. For I am convinced that nothing

*can ever separate us from his love. Death can't, and life can't. The angels won't, and all the powers of hell itself cannot keep God's love away. Our fears for today, our worries about tomorrow, or where we are—high above the sky, or in the deepest ocean—nothing will ever be able to separate us from the love of God demonstrated by our Lord Jesus Christ when he died for us.*

(Romans 8:29–39 TLB)

Make no mistake! His kingdom is here, but it is hidden. It is a spiritual kingdom. It can be seen and entered only by faith in Jesus Christ the Lord!

chapter sixteen

# God's Eternal Dimension

---

I examined the weathered grain of the gray wooden deck at my feet with magnifying-glass acuteness. Each gouge, every scrape—the hills and valleys of the boat's surface—told a story of journeys made, of waters traversed, of lives changed forever. How many other passengers had come to this shoreline? I could only imagine.

A sudden, spontaneous tingling sensation shivered down my arms. I could sense His presence. *He's here, nearby!* I remember thinking. *I dare not move.* And then I heard a familiar sound.

It was the flap of the leather case being forcefully opened. It slapped against the back of the bag, like a hand striking the firm, muscular flesh of a champion thoroughbred. The sound startled me. It came from my left, down the beach toward the entrance to the kingdom.

## Transfiguration

The light was soft and golden at first, dispelling the darkness like a candle. Jesus lifted the golden pin from the surveyor's bag. I watched with hushed reverence. I did not question. *This is too holy a moment,* I thought, realizing that to analyze would be inappropriate.

Jesus let the bag fall to the ground and held the glowing surveyor's stake out in front of Him chest high. He stared at the face of the pin for several minutes, observing His reflection in the polished length of the gleaming surface.

Finally, with a sigh of fulfillment, He turned the pin to reveal a second plane. Light began to cascade from the face of the metal. It showered Him in brilliance, revealing every aspect of His person. A hundred suns could not have generated more intensity. The spotlight of the universe was trained upon Him by the Spirit. (See John 15:26.)

> The spotlight of the universe is trained upon Jesus by the Holy Spirit.

I watched in awe, shading my squinting eyes with my hand. He was bathed in brilliance, encompassed in light. *Could this be what Peter, James, and John witnessed on the Mount of Transfiguration?* I gasped in amazement. (See Matthew 17:2.)

"I don't want this moment to end," I whispered. "I could stay here forever, inundated in this revelation of the Son of God."

Jesus turned the golden pin once more, but this time He lifted His arms like a priest holding a sacred chalice up toward heaven. The blinding intensity of the light did not deter His gaze from its glowing supremacy. A reverence cloaked His countenance like that of the high priest standing in the Holy of Holies before the ark of the covenant. And then He flung both of His hands open in surrender and let go of the sacred icon.

I groaned in horror, lunging forward instinctively with my hands outstretched to catch it. The boat rocked over on its side, spilling me onto the beach.

But the pin didn't fall!

It hung, suspended in mid-air, and then gradually began to ascend into the predawn sky. I sat perfectly still, mesmerized by what I was seeing. I could not take my eyes off the flaming pin. Its dazzling brilliance lit up the kingdom, showering the beach in a radiant luminescent gold and turning the face of the sea into an opaque, fiery-gold plane.

## Eternal, Unsolvable Mystery

Slowly, almost imperceptibly at first, the pin began to turn. Then, with steadily increasing velocity, it spun faster and faster. Cosmic showers of light poured from its glowing center, streaming out like a meteor shower in every direction. It generated a terrifying power, charging the atmosphere with creative force. The three separate surfaces of the pin were no longer distinguishable, each one dissolving into the next to form a single unbroken manifestation of God's glory and unapproachable holiness.

> Here was a single unbroken manifestation of God's glory and unapproachable holiness.

"Truly, this is the supreme absolute," I uttered, totally undone. "This final surveyor's pin of the kingdom must represent the Trinity," I declared in awe. "One God with three faces—the Son, the Spirit, and the Father—illuminating all of creation, releasing divine life, and possessing all power and authority." [1]

And then the surveyor's stake disappeared. A distant faint light replaced its incredible brilliance. The sun was rising; day was dawning in the kingdom.

## A Global Earthquake

Jesus walked toward me. "Centuries ago, Satan offered Me all the kingdoms of this world," He said. "He stated his price: 'You must fall down and worship me.' I refused. I told him, 'I will worship My Father alone. I serve Him only.' Besides, I knew his offer was premature. (See Matthew 4:8–10; Luke 4:1–13.)

"Soon, the seventh trumpet will sound. The heavenly assembly will declare the proclamation, *'The kingdoms of this world have become the kingdoms of our Lord and of His Christ, and He shall reign forever and ever!'* (Revelation 11:15 NKJV).

"Right now, the earth and the heavens are being shaken.

> The only thing that cannot be shaken is the kingdom of God.

I am removing everything that does not survive My testing. Nothing man has built can provide a place of refuge. There's no place to hide. The only thing that cannot be shaken is My kingdom. I am a consuming fire. Only those who take refuge in My kingdom will survive the days of great turmoil and fear ahead. (See Hebrews 12:25–29.)

"The end is coming soon!" He announced, staring out across the watery gulf between the invisible kingdom and the faraway world.

## The *Ekklesia*

He was gone, having vanished into the atmosphere. His final piercing words stabbed me with urgency. *The end is coming soon!*

*Where to go? What to do? I can't just stay here, secure in the kingdom, without telling others about its existence,* I thought, trembling with conviction.

I stood to brush the sand from my trousers. *The world must be told! The good news of the kingdom must be preached!*

Without hesitation, I waded into the water. Exerting all my strength, I dragged the boat from its nest in the sand toward the open sea. The bow of the ship grazed past me. My fingers skidded across the abrasive exterior of the wooden hull just above the water line. To my astonishment, something was etched into the side of the vessel. There, painstakingly carved into the plain wooden planking, were unpainted letters that I had never noticed.

*"The Ekklesia!"* I blurted out in surprised delight. "This ship is called *The Ekklesia.*" My limited knowledge of Greek served me well. *"The Church,"* I said, gratitude welling up in my heart. "It's *The Church* that got me here, and it will be *The Church* that carries me safely back to the world, where people are dying without any knowledge that there is a King and an invisible kingdom."

Dripping wet, I lunged into the boat and quickly placed the oars into their sockets. With all the energy and enthusiasm I could muster, I thrust the oars into the sea and pulled with resolve, quickly establishing a rhythm that propelled the craft forward.

Each stroke of the oars became a prayer. "Empower me by Your Spirit to be an effective servant." Another stroke. "Lord Jesus, enable me to make a difference in the world." For a long time, I

> "Jesus, let Your words be in my mouth. Let them open the eyes of the spiritually blind."

prayed and rowed. "Jesus, let Your words be in my mouth. Let them open the spiritual eyes of the blind."

The shore grew smaller with each prayer until it, too, faded into a memory. I was left with the absolute conviction that the kingdom is real. It is an unseen spiritual reality. It burned within me, consuming my thoughts and intentions. Alone, in the midst of the sea, straining at the oars of *The Church,* conviction rose in my heart. *I am a witness for the King. I am a son of the kingdom.*

A sudden sense of empowerment filled my heart. A voice—not my own—resounded within me: "Never apologize. You are an ambassador of God's kingdom; walk in that authority and power. There are miracles ahead, signs and wonders to perform in My name, diseases to heal, prisoners to release, and nations to disciple."

## A Violent Entry

A black line stretched across the approaching horizon. It looked dark and foreboding, a prison of temptations and selfish pursuits. The words of Jesus crept into my spirit. *"From the days of John the Baptist until now the kingdom of heaven suffers violence, and the violent take it by force"* (Matthew 11:12 NKJV).

"It's true, Lord. You said that it is hard for a rich man to enter the kingdom of heaven, that it is easier for a camel to go through the eye of a needle than for a rich man to enter the kingdom of God. (See Matthew 19:23–26.) Your disciples certainly asked the obvious question, *'Then who can be saved?'* (v. 25). Your response renews my hope and strengthens my faith. *'With people this is impossible, but with God all things are possible'"* (v. 26).

People who are serious about entering the kingdom are going to have to get spiritually violent. Physical birth is violent. There's nothing peaceful about the birth of a baby—screaming and yelling, pain and blood. The kingdom of God may be spiritual, but that doesn't mean it can be entered peacefully. It requires spiritual violence, a determined effort to let go of the world and overcome Satan's power.

> To enter the kingdom requires spiritual violence, a determined effort to let go of the world and overcome Satan's power.

I braced myself for a fight. A new resolve quickened my muscles. I pulled even harder upon the oars; the boat sped on toward the shore and the battle for the kingdom.

## The Grand Finale

His words echoed again in my heart: "The end is coming."

"How will it all end, Lord?" I asked.

Instantly, the Spirit drew my attention to one final Scripture:

*Then comes the end, when He hands over the kingdom to the God and Father, when He has abolished all rule and all authority and power. For He must reign until He has put all His enemies under His feet. The last enemy that will be abolished is death. For He HAS PUT ALL THINGS IN SUBJECTION UNDER His FEET. But when He says, "All things are put in subjection," it is evident that He is excepted who put all things in subjection to Him. When all things are subjected to Him, then the Son Himself also will be subjected to the One who subjected all things to Him, so that God may be all in all.*

(1 Corinthians 15:24–28)

## Back from the Well

The vision faded, and the view from my window welcomed me back to the waiting world. For weeks I had been walking with the Lord in the secret place as He revealed to me His invisible kingdom. I set my pen aside. The second golden scroll of revelation, drawn from the well of His presence, was carefully recorded in my journal. The remaining truth, which still waits to be revealed, overwhelms me.

This second golden scroll of revelation, drawn from the well of His presence, was carefully recorded in my journal.

Paul's words to the Romans express my thoughts and my heart perfectly:

*Oh, the depth of the riches both of the wisdom and knowledge of God! How unsearchable are His judgments and His ways past finding out! "For who has known the mind of the LORD? Or who has become His counselor? Or who has first given to Him and it shall be repaid to him?" For of Him and through Him and to Him are all things, to whom be glory forever. Amen.*
(Romans 11:33–36 NKJV)

# End Notes

## Acknowledgments

[1] In an appeal especially to Pentecostal or charismatic believers on this subject, Frank X. Tuoti wrote: "The masters of the spiritual life insist that the charismatic experience is a gilt-edged invitation from God to go deeper, to move beyond 'speaking in tongues' to *experiencing God in silence*." (Frank X. Tuoti, *Why Not Be a Mystic?* [New York City: Crossroad Publishing, 1998], 136).

[2] Suggested reading:

Ursula King, *Christian Mystics: The Spiritual Heart of the Christian Tradition* (New York City: Simon and Schuster, 1998).

Ursula King, *Christian Mystics: Their Lives and Legacies throughout the Ages* (Mahweh, N.J.: Hidden Spring, 2001).

Manuela Dunn Mascetti, *Christian Mysticism* (New York City: Hyperion, 1998).

The above selections trace the development of Christian mysticism from the early church to the present. In my opinion, there are some individuals included in these texts that should not be classified as purely "Christian" mystics, but I still think these resources are helpful.

[3] Frank X. Tuoti, *Why Not Be a Mystic?* (New York City: Crossroad Publishing, 1998), 23.

[4] Suggested reading:

Bob Mumford, *The King and You* (Old Tappan, N.J.: Fleming H. Revell, 1974).

George Eldon Ladd, *The Gospel of the Kingdom: Scriptural Studies in the Kingdom of God* (Grand Rapids, Mich.: Wm. B. Eerdmans Publishing Co., 1959).

E. Stanley Jones, *The Unshakable Kingdom and the Unchanging Person* (Nashville: Abingdon Press, 1972).

Geerhardus Vos, *The Teachings of Jesus Concerning the Kingdom of God and the Church* (Nutley, N.J.: Presbyterian and Reformed Publishing Co., 1972).

Richard H. Akeroyd, *The Flock and the Kingdom* (Cloverdale, Ind.: Ministry of Life, 1972).

[5] Amanda Adendorff has beautifully portrayed the four surveyor's pins of *The Hidden Kingdom* in a series of oil on canvas paintings: *Entrance into the Kingdom, The Master Key, Soil of the Heart,* and *Transfiguration.* To find out more about Amanda and her kingdom ministry and giftings as a prophetic artist, you may contact her at kingdomart1@yahoo.com.

## Introduction

[1] I highly recommend the following as an excellent reference tool:

> Leland Ryken, James C. Wilhoit, and Tremper Longman III, eds.; Colin Duriez, Douglas Penney, and Daniel G. Reid, consulting eds. *Dictionary of Biblical Imagery* (Downers Grove, Ill.: InterVarsity Press, 1998).

[2] Morton Kelsey is a prolific writer and a genuine gift to the church when it comes to spiritual direction and understanding the realm of the Spirit. All his books are worthy of careful study. For further insight regarding the nature and use of symbolism in the church, see Morton Kelsey, *Transcend: A Guide to the Spiritual Quest* (New York City: The Crossroad Publishing Company, 1981), 89.

[3] See Morton Kelsey, *Transcend: A Guide to the Spiritual Quest* (New York City: The Crossroad Publishing Company, 1981), 167.

[4] Suggested reading:

> Ken Gire, *Windows of the Soul: Experiencing God in New Ways* (Grand Rapids, Mich.: Zondervan Publishing House, 1996).

[5] Suggested reading:

> John A. Sanford, *The Kingdom Within: The Inner Meaning of Jesus' Sayings* (Mahweh, N.J.: Paulist Press, 1970).

[6] *The Hidden Kingdom: Journey into the Heart of God* is the sequel to my first book, *The Secret Place: Passionately Pursuing His Presence* (New Kensington, Pa.: Whitaker House, 2001).

## Chapter One: This Is the Air I Breathe

[1] *Breathe,* Marie Barnett. © 1995 Mercy/Vineyard Publishing/ASCAP. All rights reserved. Used by permission. Administered by Music Services, Inc.

## Chapter Two: Learning to Listen

[1] See Dr. Dale A. Fife, "The Footsteps of Enoch," chapter 4 in *The Secret Place: Passionately Pursuing His Presence* (New Kensington, Pa.: Whitaker House, 2001), 61–73.

2 Ibid., "Come to the Well," chapter 7, 103–113.

3 Ibid., "The Commission," chapter 16, 224.

4 "A minister has no more solemn duty than teaching people to wait upon God." (Andrew Murray, *Waiting on God* [New Kensington, Pa.: Whitaker House, 1981, 1983], 69.)

5 Oswald Chambers, "Vision and Darkness, January 19th," *My Utmost for His Highest Journal: Selections for the Year* (Uhrichville, Ohio: Barbour Publishing, 1935, 1963).

## Chapter Three: Willing to Wait

1 See Dr. Dale A. Fife, *The Secret Place: Passionately Pursing His Presence* (New Kensington, Pa.: Whitaker House, 2001), 115.

2 Suggested reading:

Edward W. Patton, *The Way into the Holiest: A Devotional Study of the Tabernacle in the Wilderness* (Nashville: Thomas Nelson Publishers, 1983).

C. W. Slemming, *Made According to Pattern* (Fort Washington, Pa.: Christian Literature Crusade, 1974).

C. W. Slemming, *These Are the Garments* (Fort Washington, Pa.: Christian Literature Crusade, 1974).

C. W. Slemming, *Thus Shalt Thou Serve* (Fort Washington, Pa.: Christian Literature Crusade, 1974).

3 See Exodus 25:30; 40:23; Leviticus 24:5–9.

4 Andrew Murray, *Waiting on God* (New Kensington, Pa.: Whitaker House, 1981, 1983), 25.

## Chapter Four: Priceless Gifts

1 Regarding the means of entering and leaving the well of His presence, I wrote this: "I would plunge myself into the well of His presence, and the Holy Spirit would draw me into its depths. I felt myself being lowered into the crystal-clear water. God's presence and light encompassed me. Whenever I arrived at the place of revelation He planned to give to me that day, the Holy Spirit would usher me out of the well at that level. It was like riding a spiritual elevator into the depths of God's wisdom and knowledge. Each level contained different mysteries to explore and revelations to learn." (Dr. Dale A. Fife, *The Secret Place: Passionately Pursing His Presence* [New Kensington, Pa.: Whitaker House, 2001], 131.)

2 T. S. Eliot, *Four Quartets* "Quartet #3: The Dry Salvages."

[3] Suggested reading:

> David Steindl-Rast, O.S.B., with Sharon Lebell, *The Music of Silence: Entering the Sacred Space of Monastic Experience* (San Francisco: Harper Collins, 1995).

[4] Suggested reading:

> Jim and Michal Ann Goll, *Encounters with a Supernatural God: Angelic Visitations in the Night* (Shippensburg, Pa.: Destiny Image, 1998). The second chapter is especially relevant.

## Chapter Five: The Cup of Life

[1] "Whether a man arrives or does not arrive at his destiny—the place that is peculiarly his—depends upon whether or not he finds the Kingdom within and hears the call to wholeness—or holiness, as another might say. The man who hears that call is chosen. He does not have to scramble for a place in the scheme of things. He knows that there is a place which is his and that he can live close to the One who will show it to him. Life becomes his vocation." (Elizabeth O'Conner, *Journey Inward, Journey Outward* [New York City: Harper and Row, 1968], 5.)

## Chapter Seven: The Master's Plans

[1] Suggested reading:

> John Ruskin, *The Seven Lamps of Architecture* (Mineola, N.Y.: Dover Publications, 1990).

> Steen Eiler Rasmussen, *Experiencing Architecture*, 2d. ed. (Boston, Mass.: The Massachusetts Institute of Technology, 1959, 1964).

[2] Suggested reading:

> Dr. Paul Yonggi Cho, *The Fourth Dimension* (Plainfield, N.J.: Logos International, 1979).

> Dr. Paul Yonggi Cho, with R. Whitney Manzano, *The Fourth Dimension: Volume Two, More Secrets for a Successful Faith Life*, vol. 2 (South Plainfield, N.J.: Bridge Publishing, 1984).

[3] See Dr. Dale A. Fife, *The Secret Place: Passionately Pursing His Presence* (New Kensington, Pa.: Whitaker House, 2001), 175–177.

## Chapter Eight: The Invisible Door

[1] Suggested reading:

> Jeffrey E. Post, *The National Gem Collection* (New York City: Henry N. Abrams Incorporated, 1997).

[2] Suggested reading:

>Fred Ward, *Rubies and Sapphires,* rev. ed. (Bethesda, Md.: Gem Book Publishers, 1998).
>
>C. W. Slemming, *These Are the Garments* (Fort Washington, Pa.: Christian Literature Crusade, 1974).

[3] Suggested reading:

>Fred Ward, *Rubies and Sapphires,* rev. ed. (Bethesda, Md.: Gem Book Publishers, 1998).
>
>C. W. Slemming, *These Are the Garments* (Fort Washington, Pa.: Christian Literature Crusade, 1974).

[4] Suggested reading:

>Fred Ward, *Emeralds,* 2d. ed. (Bethesda, Md.: Gem Book Publishers, 2001).

[5] Suggested reading:

>Fred Ward, *Diamonds,* rev. ed. (Bethesda, Md.: Gem Book Publishers, 1998).

[6] C. S. Lewis, *Perelandra* (New York City: Scribner, 1944, 1996), 40.

## Chapter Nine: The Narrow Pathway

[1] The kingdom and the church are not the same thing. For further information, see E. Stanley Jones, *The Unshakable Kingdom and the Unchanging Person* (Nashville: Abingdon Press, 1972), 72–73.

[2] "The church is a form which the kingdom assumes in result of the new stage upon which the Messiahship of Jesus enters with His death and resurrection." (Geerhardus Vos, *The Teaching of Jesus Concerning the Kingdom of God and the Church* [Nutley, N.J.: Presbyterian and Reformed Publishing Co., 1972], 85–86.)

[3] "It does not necessarily follow, that the visible church is the only outward expression of the invisible kingdom. Undoubtedly the kingship of God, as His recognized and applied supremacy, is intended to pervade, and control the whole of human life in all its forms of existence." (Geerhardus Vos, *The Teaching of Jesus Concerning the Kingdom of God and the Church* [Nutley, N.J.: Presbyterian and Reformed Publishing Co., 1972], 87.)

## Chapter Ten: Supernatural Keys

[1] Charles Kuralt, *A Life on the Road* (New York City: G. P. Putnam's Sons, 1990), 12.

[2] Suggested reading:

> Herman H. Riffel, *Voice of God: The Significance of Dreams, Visions, and Revelations* (Wheaton, Ill.: Tyndale House Publishers, 1978).

## Chapter Eleven: Elementary Principles

[1] The kingdom of God should not be considered as purely spiritual. It is the personal revelation of the kingdom that creates within us a desire to be a catalyst for Christ in this physical, tangible world. Jesus said that we are to be "kingdom" salt in the world, and "kingdom" light set upon a hill. We are expected to bring glory to our Father by our good works. (See Matthew 5:13–16.)

"The kingdom of God begins with the inward but doesn't stop there—it goes from what you are to what you do." (E. Stanley Jones, *The Unshakable Kingdom and the Unchanging Person* [Nashville: Abingdon Press, 1972], 164.)

[2] See Dr. Dale A. Fife, *The Secret Place: Passionately Pursing His Presence* (New Kensington, Pa.: Whitaker House, 2001), 65–70.

[3] John 14:6; 10:10; 11:25–26; 5:26, 40; 6:33 (NKJV), 48.

## Chapter Thirteen: The King's Scepter

[1] See Matthew 7:15–23; 2 Corinthians 11:13; 2 Peter 2:1.

## Chapter Fourteen: Kingdom Reflections

[1] See Luke 15:11–32 for the entire parable.

## Chapter Fifteen: The Great Mistake

[1] "Man does not put silence to the test, silence puts man to the test....Silence contains everything within itself; it is not waiting for anything, it is always wholly present in itself and completely fills out the space in which it appears." (Max Picard, *The World of Silence*, trans. Stanley Godman [Chicago, Ill.: Henry Regnery Company, 1952], 17, 22.)

[2] See Frank X. Tuoti, *Why Not Be a Mystic?* (New York City: Crossroad Publishing, 1998), 21–22.

## Chapter Sixteen: God's Eternal Dimension

[1] See Frank X. Tuoti, *Why Not Be a Mystic?* (New York City: Crossroad Publishing, 1998), 56.

# About the Author

D r. Dale Arthur Fife is a gifted pastor, author, teacher, and musician, with an insatiable passion for intimacy with God. His zeal for the Lord has led him on an incredible journey from his first pastorate of a small rural church in a coal-mining town outside of Johnstown, PA, to the cofounding of a large multiracial, inner-city church in Pittsburgh. After four decades of experience in ministry, he is now the senior pastor of a vibrant congregation in New England. His first book, *The Secret Place: Passionately Pursuing His Presence,* has blessed and encouraged thousands to seek a closer walk with Jesus.

In the mid-seventies, as a worship leader at the first outdoor Jesus Festivals, which numbered over 50,000, or in his present ministry speaking in churches, conferences, and men's and women's gatherings for leaders or intercessors, Dale's enthusiasm and hunger for God is contagious. His wisdom, maturity, and genuine spiritual concern for others have caused many to regard him as a "spiritual father" in the Lord. His insightful teaching has inspired and blessed thousands around the world.

Dr. Fife and his wife Eunice were married in 1963 and have two sons and six grandchildren. Dale graduated summa cum laude from the University of Pittsburgh. He completed seminary studies at Boston University School of Theology, and did graduate study at Pittsburgh Theological Seminary. The Doctor of Divinity degree was conferred upon him by New Life College in Bangalore, India.

Since 1988, Dale and Eunice have served as senior pastors of The Potter's House International Worship and Training Center in Farmington, Connecticut. Dale and Eunice also serve on the board of directors of The Connecticut House of Prayer and Antioch International Ministries. They are the founders of Mountain Top Ministries, a network of pastors and leaders with local, regional, and international impact. The Fifes travel throughout the world, encouraging the body of Christ to passionately pursue God's presence and proclaiming the good news of God's hidden kingdom.

Dr. Fife is available for speaking engagements upon request. He may be reached at MnTopMin@aol.com for information regarding resources, itinerary, or to schedule ministry.